WHY POETRY IN THE BIBLE MATTERS

THE CHADWICK-ODEN LECTURES

What can today's Christians learn from voices from the long history of the church in order to understand their faith in a disconnected, digitized, and divided world? This lecture series, supported by Fieldstead and Company (Irvine, California) and hosted by the Premonstratensian (Norbertine) St. Michael's Abbey (Silverado, California), was created in honor of Henry Chadwick and Thomas C. Oden and their leadership among the church and academy. Annual pairs of lectures by leading scholars and authors explore the historical and theological roots of Christianity. They apply ancient, patristic, and early medieval Judeo-Christian thought and expression that approach the faith, not simply as a collection of doctrines, but as a transformative way of life. Videos of the lecture series may be viewed at the website ChadwickOden.org.

1. *Why Does Augustine Matter?* by Rowan Williams (2023)
2. *Why Poetry in the Bible Matters*, by Robert Alter (2024)
3. *Theatrics in Patristic Preaching and Biblical Exposition*, by Paul M. Blowers (2025)

WHY POETRY IN THE BIBLE MATTERS

ROBERT ALTER

These essays are based on lectures given at St. Michael's Abbey in Silverado, California, on January 20, 2024.

Copyright © 2025 by Robert Alter, ICCS Press.

ICCS Press, Inc., 616 Prospect Street, New Haven, CT 06511 www.iccspress.com

All rights reserved. No part of this book may be reproduced in any form or by any electronic or mechanical means, including information storage and retrieval systems, without written permission from ICCS Press, except for the use of brief quotations in a book review.

Library of Congress Control Number: 2025941542

Names: Alter, Robert, author. | St. Michael's Abbey (Silverado, Calif.), host institution. | Institute for Classical Christian Studies, issuing body.
Title: Why poetry in the Bible matters . Robert Alter.
Description: New Haven, CT : ICCS Press, [2025] | Series: Chadwick-Oden lecture series.
Identifiers: LCCN: 2025941542 | ISBN: 9781624281037 (paperback) | 9781624281051 (Amazon) | 9781624281068 (ePub) | 9781624281044 (Kindle)
Subjects: LCSH: Bible. Old Testament--Language, style. | Bible. Old Testament--Criticism, interpretation, etc. | Bible--History of Biblical events--Poetry. | Hebrew poetry, Biblical--History and criticism. | Bible. Isaiah, I--Language, style. | Bible. Job, 44--Language, style. | BISAC: RELIGION / Biblical Studies / Old Testament / Poetry & Wisdom Literature. | RELIGION / Biblical Criticism & Interpretation / Old Testament.
Classification: LCC: BS1405.53 .A48 2025 | DDC: 223.06--dc23

ISBN: 978-1-62428-103-7 PB; 978-1-62428-105-1 Amazon

Printed in the United States of America on acid-free paper.

CONTENTS

1. ISAIAH	1
Author-Audience Discussion	22
2. JOB	44
Author-Audience Discussion	64
Henry Chadwick and Thomas C. Oden	77
St. Michael's Abbey	79

I

ISAIAH

Before I consider passages of poetry from Isaiah, and in my second lecture, from Job, I think it will be useful for me to provide a brief account of how the system of biblical poetry works. This is especially necessary because the formal workings of ancient Hebrew poetry continue to be imperfectly understood in the field of biblical studies, and an understanding of the system will help us understand what's going on in the poetry. Since the Oxford lectures of Bishop Robert Lowth in the mid-eighteenth century, it has been generally accepted that biblical poetry is based on semantic parallelism between the two parts (sometimes three parts) of the line, which I shall call versets. Everything, it has been assumed, works on synonymity: the poet says one thing then says it again in different words. This is sometimes more or less right, but, as I shall explain, only more or less, and the assumption of synonymity actually prevents us from following the dynamism and the plenitude of meaning that inform biblical poetry. Meanwhile, in recent decades, academics have in predictable academic fashion complicated and confused matters by proposing alternatives to parallelism. The most prevalent of these is syllable counting, which simply does not compute and which necessitates reconstructing what is claimed to be the original vowel pronunciation of the Hebrew, a rather conjectural undertaking. In sum, sadly, biblical scholars don't know much about prosody.

The most cogent account of the poetic system was articulated by the late Yale comparative literature scholar Benjamin Harshav, who was a leading authority on prosody in a range of languages, including ancient and modern Hebrew. His account, which he offered in several different versions, can most readily be found in the fourth chapter of his magisterial *Three Thousand Years of Hebrew Versification*.[1] His instructive amplification of Bishop Lowth is that there are actually three elements of parallelism in lines of biblical poetry: semantic, syntactic, and accentual. Some lines exhibit all three, some two, and some only one. The second verset of the line can replicate the syntactic pattern of the first, and it will usually have the same number of accented syllables—typically, three—as the first verset. There is no fixed requirement for the number of syllables in between the accented ones. The system thus has formal coherence and a good deal of flexibility. Finally, just as Shakespeare in his plays will from time to time for expressive purposes diverge from iambic pentameter, the Hebrew poets will occasionally bend the formal requirements of their system.

Lines of biblical poetry, preponderantly, go beyond synonymity, and that is the key to their dynamic force, as we shall see. This first dawned on me when I was teaching a graduate seminar on biblical poetry at Berkeley in the late 1970s, and I formulated this understanding in writing in my book *The Art of*

---

1. Benjamin Harshav, *Three Thousand Years of Hebrew Versification: Essays in Comparative Prosody* (New Haven, CT: Yale University Press, 2014).

Biblical Poetry.² Before its appearance, James Kugel had independently come to much the same conclusion in *The Idea of Biblical Poetry*.³ His account—"A, and what's more, B"—missed the fact that there is also often *narrative development* from the A part of the line to the B, and he compromised his valid insight by going on to insist that there is no such thing as poetry (an alien Greek business, he thought) in the Hebrew Bible, only a "continuum" from tightly parallelistic clauses to loosely parallelistic ones. The biblical writers were in fact demonstrably aware of the difference between poetry and prose, even if they had no general term for "poetry," just as they had no general term for "religion."

One essential fact about poetry should be underlined. Poetry in all systems—at least until the advent of free verse—is a kind of memory machine. Consider the function of rhyme and accentual meter in English verse. Here, for example, is the first quatrain of Shakespeare's seventy-third sonnet:

> That time of year thou mayst in me behold
> When yellow leaves, or none, or few do hang
> Upon those boughs that shake against the cold,
> Bare ruined choirs where late the sweet birds sang.⁴

Once you have "behold" in your head, you can, optimally, move surefooted to "cold" and from "hang" to "sang," the move-

---

2. Robert Alter, *The Art of Biblical Poetry* (1985; new and rev. ed., New York: Basic Books, 2011).
3. James L. Kugel, *The Idea of Biblical Poetry: Parallelism and Its History* (1981; new ed., Baltimore: Johns Hopkins University Press, 1998).
4. Shakespeare, sonnet 73 (Washington, DC: Folger Shakespeare Library, n.d.),www.folger.edu/explore/shakespeares-works/shakespeares-sonnets/read/73 (accessed November 5, 2024).

ment abetted by the regular march of iambs. The one deviation from iambic pentameter, the consecutively accented "Bare ruined," serves an expressive purpose, stressing in sound the bareness, the bleakness, of the branches that once were luxuriant with leaves. Parallelism in biblical verse has the same mnemonic force as rhyme in meter in English poetry.

Let us see how this works in one of the earliest examples of poetry in the Bible, the chant of triumph by a figure called Lamech, about whom we know nothing except the words of this poem. It begins with this line: "Adah and Zillah, O hearken my voice. / You wives of Lamech, give ear to my speech" (Gen. 4:23–24).[5] Here all three of the components of parallelism are present in perfect symmetry: "Adah and Zillah" / "wives of Lamech"; "hearken" / "give ear"; "voice" / "speech." The second half of the line mirrors the syntax of the first half, and the Hebrew has four beats in each of the versets. If this were true everywhere in biblical poetry, parallelism would explain everything. But Lamech's poem concludes: "For sevenfold Cain is avenged, / and Lamech seventy and seven." If synonymity ruled, we would expect something like "and Lamech three plus four." But, invariably, if a number appears in the first half of the line, it has to go up—by a decimal place or more, by one, or by a decimal place plus the initial number. Here is an exemplary line from the Song of Moses: "O how could one chase a thousand, / and two put ten thousand to flight?" (Deut. 32:30). Numbers are the revealing schematic instance of a process repeatedly working through the line in biblical poetry. As we move from the first verset to the second, utterance is intensified: general statements become specific, abstract terms are concretized, overviews become close focuses, and if spatial entities are involved, we go from large to

---

5. All Bible translations in this book are my own, published as *The Hebrew Bible: A Translation with Commentary*, 3 vols. (New York: W. W. Norton, 2018).

small or outside to inside (house to room). Through all this, the attentive reader will find that surprising things happen. Consider another line from the Song of Moses: "He suckled him honey from the crag, / and oil from the flinty stone" (Deut. 32:14). The first half of the line could make sense naturalistically: a people wandering through wasteland might conceivably come upon beehives in the crevices of rocks. But the second half of the line turns God's provenance into something miraculous—olive oil does not come out of a stone, and, note, in a characteristic second-verset move, we are taken from rocks to a particular kind of rock, and one that is specially hard, the flintstone. All this is like the move from a thousand to ten thousand, but without the numbers.

This dynamic is equally manifested in erotic poetry. In the Song of Songs 8:1, the young woman says to her beloved: "Would that you were a brother to me, / suckling my mother's breasts." Now, the poet is faced with a challenge: having said "brother" in the initial verset, he needs a synonym for it in the second, but there is none in Biblical Hebrew as there is none in modern English. If it were possible to say "male sibling" in the ancient language, that would certainly not serve in poetry. But "suckling my mother's breasts" is more than just an ad hoc synonym for "brother." It is a very physical and distinctly sensual indication of fraternity that intimates the sexual encounter she has in mind, where he will press his lips to her breasts, not her mother's. One could scarcely find a better example of how in the seeming repetition of the second half of the line there is development, something is happening.

As we turn to the poetry of Isaiah, we should first ask, why did the prophets speak in poetry? They did not always: there are extended prose passages in Jeremiah and Ezekiel as well as in the minor prophets. But Isaiah the son of Amoz, the first of the three remarkable poets whom tradition has grouped together in the Book of Isaiah, prefers poetry throughout. There are two obvious explanations for this, though the second will be more relevant to our purposes. First, it is God who is represented as speaking, something explicitly noted by the introduction of many of the prophecies with the so-called messenger formula, "Thus said the LORD." This is the same formula used for human messages in ancient Israel. If I sent you a letter in a scroll, the heading at the top would read, "Thus said Robert Alter." Given that these are proffered as God's words, it is perfectly appropriate that they should be cast in elevated language, which is to say, poetry. Beyond the appropriateness for divine speech, because of the mnemonic function of poetry that I observed at the outset, prophetic poetry is a vehicle for strongly imprinting in the memory of its auditors the message that the prophet means to convey to them: "Woe, offending nation, / people weighed down with crime" (1:4). Once you hear the first half of the line, as with rhyme, you are likely to remember the second half as well. And given the logic of intensification that governs biblical poetry the emphasis of castigation gets stronger: from the general term *offending*, the poem moves on to a physical sense of crime as a weight bearing down on the people. Even what looks to the casual eye like bland synonymity proves to be something more: "The ox knows its owner, / and the donkey its master's stall" (1:3). The initial verset declares the general idea of ownership of the beast. In the more concrete second half, we zoom in to the stall, where the master provides feed for his animal, which then leads us to the prophet's compelling idea that though God has provided sustenance for his people, they, unlike the dumb beast, behave as though they did not know the hand that fed them.

    I would now like to look at a few extended examples of how the impressive poetry of this prophet works to serve the ends of prophecy. Here is his denunciation in verse of the turpitude of Jerusalem's population:

> How has the faithful town
>   become a whore?
> Filled with justice,
>   where righteousness did lodge,
>   and now—murderers.
> Your silver has turned to dross,
>   your drink is mixed with water.
> Your nobles are knaves
>   and companions of thieves.
> All of them lust for bribes
>   and chase illicit payments.
> They do not defend the orphan,
>   and the widow's case does not touch them.
>
> (1:21–23)

Although whoredom is more typically used in biblical literature as a metaphor for idolatry—betraying the covenantal bond with God by dallying with foreign gods—Isaiah employs it for perversion of justice, his overriding concern. The Hebrew word *zonah* is not coarse or obscene, but it is certainly blunt, and so my translation avoids a more decorous English synonym such as "harlot." The second line of poetry here is triadic, and lines with three parts are often deployed to mark in the third verset a sharp transition or contrast: after the former condition of "justice" and "righteousness"—"murderers," an abrupt clause without a verb, only this violent noun. I am not sure whether Isaiah is referring to actual killings or simply to outrages perpetrated on the helpless. One recalls his denunciation of people who come into the Temple bringing sacrifices with blood on their hands. I suspect that if he were prophesying in our own society, he would label as murder the violation of moral concern in the inner cities through the failure to provide shelter and medical care.

Sound-play reinforces his poetic argument. The turning of silver to dross is emphasized by the alliterative link between the two words, *kaspeikh, siggim*. This move is allied with a linguistic device Isaiah favors and uses with great dexterity, which is to join together two words that sound alike but are antithetical in meaning, the first positive and the second negative. It is a way of vividly conveying through language the total reversal of decency in the kingdom of Judah. A striking example is the second line of poetry in 5:2: "He [God] hoped for justice, and, look, jaundice, / for righteousness, and, look, wretchedness." The Hebrew for "justice" is *mishpat* and for "jaundice" is *mispaḥ*. The second term actually means "blight," but I thought that it was essential to reproduce the wordplay of the original in order to retain the sharp thrust of the Hebrew—and jaundice, after all, is a kind of blight. The second verset is definitely stronger in the Hebrew, moving from *tsedaqah*, "righteousness," to *tseʿaqah*, "a scream," this abrupt introduction of violence (somewhat like "murderers" above) unfortunately lacking in my English equivalent. In the passage cited from chapter 1, the alliterative antithetical terms, "nobles," knaves," reflects a fuller alliteration in the Hebrew, *sarayikh* and *sorerim*. One readily sees how this artful manipulation of language forcefully drives home the castigation. The other feature of this passage that should be noted is how it advances, rather like the focusing movement within the line of poetry, from the general or metaphoric to the specific. How is the knavery of the nobles manifested? They are companions of thieves. And what chicanery, concretely, have they been up to? Bribery, raking in illicit payments, failing to defend the widow and the orphan. These in Israelite society, along with resident aliens, have no legal protection and so are desperately in need of the powerful to plead their cause. In all this, the medium of poetry is deftly wielded as a weapon to stab the conscience of the audience that the prophet seeks to turn back from their corrupt behavior.

The broader rhetorical strategy of prophetic poetry is to conjure up in concrete and dismaying imagery what the prophet believes will be the dire consequences for a society that has perverted justice—the so-called prophecies of doom. There are abundant instances of such prophecies in Isaiah. I will illustrate from chapter 2, where the doom-saying takes up the last sixteen of the twenty-two verses of the chapter. It is too long to quote in full, but here is a substantial segment:

> And the human shall bow low
> and man shall be brought down.
> And do not spare them!
> Come into the crag
> and hide in the dust
> for the fear of the Lord
> and from His pride's glory.
> The eyes of human haughtiness are brought down
> and men's righteousness is bowed low,
> and the Lord alone shall be raised high
> on that day.
> For it is a day of the Lord of Armies,
> over all the proud and lofty
> and over all on high and lifted up.
> And over all the Lebanon cedars
> that are lofty and raised high
> and over all the Bashan oaks,
> and over all the lofty mountains
> and over all the raised-up mountains,
> and over every looming tower

>   and over every fortress wall,
>   and over all the Tarshish ships
>   and over all lovely crafts.
>   And human haughtiness shall bow low
>   and men's loftiness be brought down,
>   and the LORD alone shall be exalted
>   on that day.
>   And the ungods shall utterly vanish.
>   And they shall come into caves in the crags
>   and into hollows in the dust
>   from the fear of the LORD
>   and from His pride's glory
>   when He rises to wreak havoc on earth.
>   (2:9–19)

These lines employ a strategy that is fairly unusual in biblical poetry. A single controlling image runs through the whole extended sequence: man, who presumed to set himself on high, is dashed to the earth, brought utterly low, while God looms on high. The poem proceeds in a cascading flow of images of high and low, with Isaiah exploiting the biblical fondness for parataxis in the long series of items on high linked by one *and* after another, all to be brought low. Height is of course a metaphor for lofty position in society and in what we would call the power structure, and it might refer as well to actual buildings higher than the habitations of the poor, perhaps to residences on the heights of the city. The Lebanon cedars are a recurrent phrase for height in biblical literature—Israel was poor in forests with tall trees, and one recalls that Solomon had to import cedars from Lebanon for his construction projects. Toward the end of the catalog, the list segues to fortifications—looming towers and fortress walls. These will prove of no avail, and so the destruction of the city by an enemy is implied.

What is notable in the poetic structure of the passage as a whole is that it extends the dynamic of the single line. In fact, because it is a catalog, the movement of intensification within the line is replaced by simple semantic parallelism of similar items (Lebanon cedars and Bashan oaks, looming towers and fortress walls). Instead, the intensification plays out through the larger sequence, reinforced through the sheer accumulation of items in the catalog. At the end, we get a repetition of the image of people cowering in crags and hollows in terror of divine wrath that appeared at the beginning. What is added climactically at the conclusion is the fearsome "when He rises to wreak havoc on earth." Poetry in prophecies such as this is a vehicle to strike terror in the hearts of the people listening to it. First, in chapter 1, we had the prophet's denunciation of the people's moral transgressions ("All of them lust for bribes / and chase illicit payments"), and now he conjures up the terrible retribution that will be exacted for their actions. Poetry with its impulse for concreteness serves as an instrument to depict a landscape of disaster, the decidedly dark side of prophetic vision. As people scurry to hide in holes and crevices, God is imagined sweeping over the land, raining down destruction. Note how a triadic line is used to strongly mark the conclusion, the third member of the line introducing the culminating summary of disaster, "when He rises to wreak havoc on earth."

Before turning to an antithetical phase of prophecy, I would like to consider a different kind of poetic catalog. It should be said that catalogs in poetry and other literary works are by no means anomalous. We recall—perhaps not with relish for everyone—the catalog of ships in the *Iliad*. Rabelais abounds in catalogs. In Joyce's *Ulysses* we have the catalog of the contents of Leopold Bloom's pockets near the end and quite a few other catalogs along the way. Catalogs have a certain appeal to the imagination because they embody the material presence and nature of a particular slice of reality. And so, in chapter 3, which in the canonical arrangement follows the vision of the haughty brought low, Isaiah comes back from the landscape of apocalypse to the streets of Jerusalem that he actually walked, now evoking the elegant ladies of the city parading in their finery. This passage has often been accused of misogyny, but after quoting it, I would like to propose a different way of conceiving what might motivate it. The prophecy is introduced by the formulaic "And the Lord said," thus attributing to God the harshly judgmental perception of the women that follows.

> And the Lord said:
>   Since Zion's daughters are haughty.
>   and they walk with necks thrust forth
>   and with wanton eyes,
>   walking with mincing steps
>   and jingling with their feet,
> the Master shall blight the pates of Zion's daughters
>   and expose their private parts.
> On that day the Master shall take away
>   the splendid ankle bells and the headgear
>   and the crescents and the pendants
>   and the bracelets and the veils
> and the necklaces and the armlets
>   and the sashes and the amulets and the charms,
> the finger-rings and the nose-rings,
>   the robes and the wraps and the shawls and the purses,
> and the gowns and the draped cloths
>   and the turbans and the capes.
> For instead of perfume, rot shall be,

>   and instead of sashes, rope,
>   and instead of beaten-work, baldness,
>   and instead of rich robes, girding of sackcloth,
>   for instead of beauty, shame. (3:16–24)

We have not retained the lexicon of ancient Israelite haute couture and the accoutrements of fashion, so the translation of quite a few items in the list involves educated guesses, though the general sense is not in doubt. The long catalog of details of fashion and female ornamentation is, we might say, parataxis on steroids, with emphasis achieved through sheer accumulation. The cumulative effect is bolstered by anaphora in the repeated "instead of." The angry thrust of the prophecy is amplified by the placement at the end of the versets the sundry grim things that will come instead of the finery ("rope," "baldness," "sackcloth"). Sound also has a role in the force of the words, as in the blunt monosyllable for "rot," *maq,* which is then linked by alliteration with *niqpah,* the word for "rope." These women, moreover, intend not just to look good but to be sexually alluring: the wanton eyes and the mincing steps suggest that the fashion display is a prelude to sex.

To see this invective as more than sheer antipathy toward women, I would like to invoke an analogy I used in the commentary on this passage in my translation of the Hebrew Bible. Imagine a twenty-first-century Isaiah walking west in Midtown Manhattan from First Avenue to Madison Avenue. On his way he passes homeless people huddled in their rags against building facades or hunkered down on the sidewalk in shabby sleeping bags. Then, on Madison Avenue, he sees women emerging from the elegant boutiques in their designer dresses and coats, with bags emblazoned with the names of the boutiques filled to the top with new acquisitions. He responds with a surge of enraged indignation: all this conspicuous consumption and preening self-indulgence done in a city where the widow and the orphan and the unemployed are shamefully neglected and wealth is monopolized by the one percent. This, I imagine, is more or less what Isaiah walking through the streets in the late decades of the seventh century B.C.E. would have felt when he framed this fierce poem. I would not rule out some general hostility toward women that might animate these words, but I suspect that the dominant motive is social indignation. The passage does not reflect the typical shape of prophetic poetry, but it does take advantage of poetry's power to enable us to visualize concrete realities in order to articulate a plea for the urgent necessity for a more just social order.

At the outset, I mentioned the generally overlooked aspect of narrativity that often manifests itself in the dynamic of lines of biblical poetry, but it happened not to be on display in the passages so far considered. I would therefore like to highlight narrativity in three different lines from Isaiah that demonstrate its force in prophetic poetry. In 5:26, which is part of the evocation of a terrifying enemy that will descend on the kingdom of Judah riding battle horses and wielding arms, we encounter the following triadic line: "And He shall raise a banner from afar / and whistle to one at the ends of the earth, / and, look, swiftly, quick, he shall come."

A miniature story unfolds through the three parts of the line, and that is why the poet needs three rather than the usual two versets. God is figured as a commanding general. In the first of the three versets, he raises a banner to signal to the distant troops to prepare to charge. In the second verset, he emits a piercing whistle that orders the troops to begin their advance. In the third verset, the swift charge is launched. Note that in all this the alien troops are God's army, following His military command. This scary narrative continues through the lines that follow: no one tires in the ranks of the foe; not even a sandal comes undone; all their arrows are sharpened, their bows drawn, the pounding hooves of their horses are like flintstone, the wheels of their chariots like the whirlwind. This dramatic martial poetry palpably imposes on its listeners a frightening vision of impending doom.

Just before this in the same prophecy (5:25), we see a more common deployment of narrativity within the line. It is part of this whole evocation of God unleashing devastating punishment on his derelict people: "And mountains have quaked, / and their corpses are become like offal in the streets." First there is a cataclysmic upheaval in the mountains around Jerusalem, and then in the second half of the line we see the results of the earthquake—corpses strewn over the streets of the city.

Finally, in a prophecy that spells out Israel's tense waiting for God's saving intervention (26:17), we have "As a woman with child draws near to give birth, / she shudders, she shakes in her pangs, / so we were before you, O LORD." In the first verset, the woman feels the initial signs of the onset of labor; in the second, she is in the midst of the throes of the birth pangs. The poet then uses the last verset to break from parallelism and execute a kind of pivot, as often happens at the end of triadic lines—here to make explicit that the scene of birthing is a metaphor for the people's anxious dependence on God. "We were with child, we shuddered, as if birthing the wind," the poem continues in the next line. But the birth metaphor implies that something good will come out of this anguish.

I have taken the trouble to trace the temporal movement forward within these three lines to illustrate a general principle. The prophets were of course not poets in the "professional" sense that Homer or Sappho or Virgil were, or other writers dedicated to producing poems to entertain or to please audiences with beautifully crafted words. Yet by instinct and inclination and natural gifts, the prophets at their verbal best, like Isaiah the son of Amoz, were nevertheless poets. They obviously were familiar with the formal workings of their culture's Hebrew poetry, and they had an excellent sense of how to marshal its resources for the purposes of prophecy. Poetry, they understood, was a mnemonic, a persuader, a vehicle for making ideas palpable to the imagination, and that is why they felt it was an appropriate instrument for driving home to the people the urgent words of God. The deployment of narrativity within the line is one small instance of how the established procedures of Hebrew poetry served the ends of prophecy, making the prophecies gripping to those who heard them.

If biblical poetry were restricted to gloom, doom, and invective—as is the case of the passages reviewed here so far—it is unlikely that it would speak to contemporary readers as it still does. But there are also, of course, luminous prophecies of hope and consolation, and in those radiant evocations of a better time to come, the resources of poetry play an equally important role in conveying the vision. Let me quote just a few lines from the famous imagining of a grand future redemption in Isaiah 11:

> And the wolf shall dwell with the lamb,
>   and the leopard lie down with the kid.
> And the calf and the lion shall feed together,
>   a little lad leading them.
> And the cow and the bear shall graze,
>   together their young shall lie,
>   and the lion like cattle eat hay.
> And an infant shall play by a viper's hole,
>   and on an adder's den
>   a babe put forth his hand.
> They shall do no evil nor act ruinously
>   in all My holy mountain.

> For the earth shall be filled with knowledge of the LORD
> as water covers the sea. (11:6–9)

What we see here is not really a poetic catalog, like the two we have looked at, but rather parallelism within the line mirrored by interlinear parallelism. A large part of Israelite economy in this era involved sheep-herding, goat-herding, and cattle-herding, and beasts of prey were a constant threat, as we learn in the David story when he says that as a young shepherd he has killed lion and bear. Note in the second line above how there is a break in semantic parallelism as the poet focuses in the second half of the line on the "little lad" leading the herbivore and the carnivore together, a vivid image of the harmonious new age. In the next line, which is triadic, the third verset is used for a striking effect of concretization: after the more general reference to feeding and grazing, we are invited to envisage the utopian (and virtually absurd) moment of the lion eating hay. In the following line, the image of the babe is extended in the sharp focus on the infant playing by the viper's hole and the hand of the babe reaching out over the den of the adder—in the future ideal age, even the most innocent and vulnerable will be able to play alongside what once were lethal creatures. The third verset of this line is used, characteristically for triadic lines—"a babe put forth his hand"-- to introduce a kind of cinematic close-up in the parallelism. The Hebrew of this line, I should add, shows a small progression that unfortunately cannot be transposed into readable English. The word for "infant," *yoneq*, literally means "suckling," and the one for "babe" means "weaned child," so even rather casually, there is a movement forward in time from the first verset to the second.

What did the prophet mean to say through these extravagant images? Traditionally, both Christians and Jews have read this passage and others like it eschatologically. The grand flourish of the final verset in the passage quoted—not a parallel utterance but a fine simile for how the knowledge of God will cover the earth "as water covers the sea"—reinforces the sense of eschatology. In this view, the prophet is foreseeing an age in which history and even the animal kingdom will be radically transformed so that the very beasts of prey will turn gentle and harmless in a reign of universal peace and harmony, which is to say, the messianic age. I doubt that Isaiah, a keen observer of behavior in his own city, actually thought a time would come when the laws of nature would change and predation cease from the earth, with lions eating hay. And we should remember that *messiah*, a word that does not appear in this particular passage but in others, was in this era still a political term meaning "the anointed one." It designated the person who has gone through the prescribed ritual of anointment that confirmed him as the legitimate ruler. Isaiah 11 envisages an ideal future king who will rule a nation where universal justice prevails, and that is the force of these hyperboles.

The logic of the biblical poetic system pushes toward hyperbole through the prevalent dynamic of intensification from the first half of the line to the second. A line from Deuteronomy 32, quoted earlier, is instructive in regard to the transformation of nature in our passage. As we saw, the first verset there expresses a naturalistic possibility, finding honeycombs in rock crevices, whereas the second verset, as the parallelism of meaning is stepped up, gives us miraculous oil from the flintstone. What I would say is that the penchant of biblical poetry for hyperbole prepares the way for eschatology, offering texts not originally eschatological that will readily lend themselves to later eschatological readings. In some of the ostensibly eschatological passages, though not in what I've quoted, the expression *aḥarit hayamim* appears. It has often been translated as "the end of days," which is what it came to mean in later Hebrew, but what it originally meant is "the aftertime," that is, sometime in the future. *Aḥarit* derives from the preposition *aḥar*, "after."

Let me add just one more example of a prophecy of redemption from chapter 40. It is by a different prophet from Isaiah the son of Amoz, as scholarship long ago decisively concluded. This prophet spoke decades later in the Babylonian exile, addressing the exiles, attempting to encourage them in their dejection to return to their land. There is no sign of the moral castigation so prominent in the original Isaiah, and his poetry, fine in its own way, reads quite differently. Jewish tradition appropriately adopts seven passages from his prophecies to be chanted in synagogue on the seven Sabbaths after the fast of Tisha B'Av, when the destruction of the Temple and Jerusalem is mourned. As to the inclusion of this prophet in the Book of Isaiah, we should keep in mind that biblical texts were literally open books, that the work of later writers could be added to a scroll if it seemed somehow in keeping with the original text. The Book of Isaiah would surely be diminished if the splendid poetry of this anonymous prophet of the exile were not part of it.

> Comfort, O comfort My people,
>   says your God.
> Speak to the heart of Jerusalem
>   and call out to her,
> for her time of service is ended,
>   her crime is expiated,
> for she has taken from the LORD's hand
>   double for all her offenses.
> A voice calls out in the wilderness:
>   Clear a way for the LORD's road,
>   level in the desert a highway for our God!
> Every valley shall be lifted high

>   and every mountain brought low,
> and the crooked shall be straight,
>   and the ridges become a valley.
> And the Lord's glory shall be revealed, and
>   all flesh together shall see
>   that the Lord's mouth has spoken. (40:1–5)

The prophecy is not introduced by the set formula "Thus said the Lord." Instead, the very first words are an imperative verb, conjugated in the plural, and evidently addressed to people in general or to the nations (though there is interpretive dispute about whom is addressed). This pliant introduction of divine speech might reflect the fluidity with which biblical literary conventions were beginning to be used in the sixth century B.C.E. The exiled people need comforting, and the repeated "comfort" is the first word they hear. "Term of service" (*tzava'*) is a kind of prison sentence, but the crime for which it was imposed has now been expiated after a double punishment. (One of the more unfortunate errors of the King James Version is to render this noun as "army," a meaning it has elsewhere.) The voice calling in the wilderness has become, understandably, proverbial, but its original formulation here is quite literal. The exiles, looking across to the west over a rugged and desolate landscape of several hundred miles, may well be daunted by the prospect of trekking back to Zion, a return perhaps made possible by a decree of the Persian emperor Cyrus, who has conquered the Babylonians. The prophet needs to encourage his fellow exiles to undertake the arduous journey back to their homeland. He does this, as we might expect in biblical poetry, through hyperbole, though a somewhat different kind of hyperbole from what we saw in Isaiah 11. It seems unlikely that he actually thought that hundreds of miles of wasteland would be leveled for the exiles and that a highway would miraculously appear in the rugged terrain. In fact, it's unlikely that his audience took him literally because they were, after all, being urged to set out on the journey in the immediate future, not in some far-off time, and what would they think if they then found no highway in the wilderness? What these stirring lines do is to conjure up a hopeful vision: whatever your fears, you will find a way back, the return to Zion will prove easy, you will march through the wilderness as though it had turned level and smoothed out before you, and that very passage will manifest God's glory, His providential concern for His people. The prophecy concludes with the confirmation of its source, "the LORD's mouth has spoken," paired with "says your God" at the beginning in a way that diverges from the set formula for signaling divine speech.

It should be evident why this prophet of the exile makes poetry the vehicle for his message of exhortation and comfort. Poetry, as we have seen, reinforces memory, and there is surely much that is memorable in these lines, something attested to by the fact that a hundred generations of readers, in the Hebrew and in translation, have kept a good deal of it in memory. But poetry is also an instrument of persuasion, and if anything could move the hesitant exiles to embark on the challenging return to their land, it would be this rousing vision of the crooked made straight, of God's highway spanning the wilderness. What is true of the prophecies of hope and consolation is true of the prophecies that issue withering condemnation and dire warnings. Poetry was certainly not an aesthetic exercise for Isaiah or for any of the other prophets, but it offered a medium that could powerfully convey messages intended to be persuasive, whether encouragement, exhortation, or denunciation, and the biblical prophets employed the many formal resources of poetry with great dexterity and imagination to achieve their prophetic ends. Attention to how their poems worked as poems brings us closer to what they meant to say and to why it exerts the power it does.

AUTHOR-AUDIENCE DISCUSSION

AUDIENCE MEMBER: Is it true that there is no poetry in the New Testament?

ROBERT ALTER: Well, I wouldn't say that. In Revelation, it's not poetry, but I would say prose poetry. It's very heavy in imagery, some of it quite striking.

AUDIENCE MEMBER: And if Job was poetic in poetry, why is it that God didn't choose the Passion of Christ to be poetic?

ROBERT ALTER: One thing that I would say is that the Gospel writers wanted Jesus' humanity to be powerfully present to their readers or listeners. For example, when Jesus before the crucifixion says, "Let this cup pass from me." Or even when he quotes a line of poetry, which is actually a line of Psalms, on the cross, and He says—actually, he quotes it in Aramaic, *Eli, Eli, lama sabachthani?* which means, "My God, my God, why have you forsaken me?" I suspect that this humanization of the Christ figure might have been harder to convey in the elevated diction of poetry. Anybody who wants to add to that can.

AUDIENCE MEMBER: There is a tradition that he was reciting a whole Psalm 22 when he said, "My God, my God," so there's some that will be a prayer song.

Audience member: People like C. S. Lewis and Tolkien talked about "true myth." You know, wonderful stories that were true. For there was a real man who lived a real life and died on a real cross. And that's hard.

Robert Alter: Yeah, that's what I think.

Audience member: I was just thinking on that note, too, there's this one passage where Jesus talks about straining a gnat and swallowing a camel. I don't know Aramaic very well, but I've heard that if you back-translate that, it's straining *algama* and swallowing *algama*. And so Jesus is being poetic in that sense, as well.

Audience member: I have just returned from a study tour to Egypt. And so across the canvas of my mind is parading all the things I saw in tombs and on temple walls. And so as we were looking at chapter 11, all these animals: wolf, lamb, leopard, calf, lion—what I'm envisioning, and wondering if this could be a connection point is in the tomb of Rekhmire, who was a vizier of Thutmosis III and Amenhotep II, there's lines and lines of foreigners bringing tribute to the king, and they're bringing a giraffe and a cheetah and baboons and all these different animals. And I'm wondering if there's a possibility, if we're looking at this as an anointed king who will bring about this kind of justice, could it be that the animals are representing nations that are living at peace together who represent different kinds of animals? And then the second part of my question is, I can't help but notice that it's snakes and snake holes that the infant is putting his hand near. And all the Egyptian iconography has snakes in it, representing royal authority. And so do you think this child, the infant, is the Anointed King who is bringing about this kind of justice? And is that symbolized by him being able to put his hand by the snake? Or am I just making things up?

ROBERT ALTER: I'm a bit skeptical. I think, these are just ravenous beasts selected from the animal kingdom, and they're not symbolic or allegorical.

AUDIENCE MEMBER: Is the child the ruler who's bringing about this kind of peace or is the child experiencing the results of that rule?

ROBERT ALTER: I think the latter. That is, in the peaceful kingdom of the future, even the lethal forces of nature no longer exert themselves as lethal. So a small child could play by an adder's den and in no way be harmed. I think that's all it is.

AUDIENCE MEMBER: I think of the parables of Christ as being very poetic in the sense that they were not talking about rhyming particularly, but the way that they will bring two diverse images. You know, you talked earlier about "seeing" in poetry. Someone mentioned this. Instead of reading, in a way we have this visual when we study poetry, a vivid visual comes and it doesn't always explain itself. And Jesus didn't always explain his parables. He set them out there for contemplation and for discovery to happen through the juxtaposition of these different images, like the seed and the sower, and just over and over, he used visual imagery that was not prose. It was not storytelling. It was putting things together for you to contemplate. And that to me is quite poetic.

Robert Alter: There's a general sense in which "poetic" as an adjective is used. And that's any verbal constellation that does for us, as the readers, something fairly similar to what we experience in reading poetry, we say is poetic. And I get that. I don't dismiss that. But what I've been talking about in these lectures is poetry as a formal system. In the Hebrew Bible that formal system consists usually of two parts of a line with three beats, three accented syllables, in each half of the line, and some kind of developing similarity in meaning, or sometimes an antithetical meaning, between the first half and the second half. I mean, that's as clear-cut as when you're reading a text in English and all of a sudden in the middle of a prose narrative, you have six lines that scan perfectly as iambic pentameter, and there's an *ABABAB* rhyme pattern in the six lines. So when I'm talking about the force of poetry, I'm talking about the formal system. It's true that the parables are open in meaning. They're evocative, they can be haunting. And all those things are definitely related to what we experience in reading poetry, but it's like—oh, let's say—I was talking about novels over lunch with somebody, Faulkner's *Absalom, Absalom!* which I definitely consider to be the greatest American novel written in the twentieth century. The language is sometimes amazing and extraordinarily evocative. But we wouldn't say that *Absalom, Absalom!* is a novel written in verse. That is where I stand.

AUDIENCE MEMBER: I've always been intrigued by the language of the "fear of the Lord" in the Hebrew Bible. The verse that comes first to mind is "The fear of the Lord is the beginning of wisdom." I'd love to hear you talk a little bit about the way that poetry or sort of poetic speech maybe is or isn't functioning in language around the fear of the Lord.

ROBERT ALTER: Okay. First of all, the phrase "fear of the Lord," one must grant, could mean, in some contexts, being afraid of God. But mostly, it doesn't. Mostly, it means something like "recognizing God's power, holding God in extreme reverence." In later Hebrew, for example, the same word connected with *shamayim,* "heaven," in the often used in the phrase *yirat shamayim*, "fear of heaven," means something like "piety." It doesn't mean that you're in a state of fear. But, actually, the prophetic poetry of castigation is often about fear in the other sense. The prophet in fact wants to make his listeners afraid. That is, since his theological assumption, which we may or may not share—that evil deeds end up being punished and that catastrophes will befall the people of Israel if they continue to behave in an immoral or paganizing way—is a theology especially rooted in the Book of Deuteronomy. The prophet, given that assumption, in a way wants to strike terror in the hearts of those who are listening to his poetry. And so he conjures up all these images—like that one line that I quoted about God raising a banner on high and whistling to an enemy from the ends of the earth who comes galloping down against Israel—I think that's really designed to make people quake in their boots, or in their sandals. And so that is where fear plays into prophetic poetry. And the flip side of it is that most of the prophets do have a balancing vision of redemption like the one we saw in chapter 11.

ISAIAH

AUDIENCE MEMBER: I'm just curious because I know you know modern Hebrew. Does modern Hebrew poetry pick up on the ancient Hebrew poetry? Does it use the same forms? Or does it do something else?

ROBERT ALTER: I should say for the information of the audience that modern Hebrew literature actually is another area in which my wandering interests have focused, and I love modern Hebrew poetry and do a lot with Hebrew fiction, as well. The form definitely is not the same. That is, the forms of modern Hebrew poetry are pretty much borrowed from the European and American repertoire, especially, early twentieth-century European poetry. There are a lot of poems that are composed following Russian models, including the meters used by the Russian poets. Some meters, we don't know at all in English, like one called "amphibrachs"—which is a poetic unit, a metric foot, of unstressed, stressed, unstressed—we don't have that in English at all. And then free verse entered Hebrew, in particular, following American and English models. So formally, it is not like the Bible. In other ways, the Bible is very present in modern Hebrew poetry because it is such a rich and powerful reservoir of poetry that poets dip into it all the time. And biblical allusions are all over the place. I like a little poem by the great Hebrew poet Yehuda Amichai, who died twenty-four years ago—he was a dear friend—which is called "God's Fate." I will recite to you in translation. It's very short, so I'm not committing one of these spectacular memory feats that I talked about. I wish I could.

> God's fate now
> is like the fate
> of trees and stones, sun and moon,

> when people stopped believing in them
> and began to believe in him.
>
> But he has to stay with us:
> at least like the trees, like the stones
> and the sun and the moon and the stars.[6]

What the poem is obviously alluding to is the wood, or the sacred trees, and the stones in prophetic denunciations of idolatry. But then, the sun and the moon and the stars as they appear here take us back to Genesis 1, the words of which Amichai recalls textually. This is a small illustration of how alive the language and imagery of the Bible remain in the imagination of a modern Hebrew poet.

AUDIENCE MEMBER: I have a quick question concerning Biblical Hebrew and the interpretation of it with respect to the cultural aspects. Do you have a good reference document for the interpretation of Biblical Hebrew taking into consideration the cultural aspects?

ROBERT ALTER: I don't think there's one book or article that does that. But what's happened is, beginning in the later nineteenth century, archeologists unearthed a whole world that we didn't know about, much of which was the cultural context of ancient Israel. This has been absorbed by Bible scholars and has entered in multifarious ways into the commentaries and articles that they have written on biblical books. So, say, you read any

---

6. My translation, in *The Poetry of Yehuda Amichai,* edited by Robert Alter (New York: Farrar, Straus & Giroux, 2015).

volume of the Anchor Bible—it started off with Doubleday, it's now published by Yale University Press, and it's the most prominent recent scholarly commentary in English on the Bible. Each volume is done by a different scholar. You will find in those volumes swarms of references to the ancient cultural context uncovered by archeologists. The Anchor Bible Exodus is particularly good. The Anchor Bible, of course, is inevitably uneven because it is the work of different people. The Anchor Bible Samuel, for example, by Kyle McCarter, is excellent. Finally, after thirty-five years, my dear friend and colleague Ron Hendel is coming out with the first volume of his Genesis. And that's going to be really good.

AUDIENCE MEMBER: You had said in response to one of the questions that most of the time the Jewish writers of these biblical times aren't that interested in nature? And so I wanted to ask, what were they interested in as it seems to you, and then also, I wanted to know what made you say that because I was just thinking like the Psalms are just chock full of nature images, or like Isaiah, the imagery of the rain is all over the place in there and the dirt, the salty land becoming a beautiful land.

ROBERT ALTER: There is definitely imagery of rain, growing things, vineyards. But what you don't have is very much truly descriptive poetry evoking the concrete presence of things in the natural world, which is why I said that, and biblical narrative, as I'm sure you are aware, is not very descriptive at all. And since you asked, "What replaces nature," I would say language. I have become especially conscious of the crucial role of language in the culture because I've recently been working on a short book on dialogue in the Bible. And at least in the narratives from the beginning of Genesis through at least the early chapters of Kings, anything important that takes place in the story switches from narrative report—and the narration is often brutally summarizing—to dialogue. You have, for example, seventeen years of Moses's life as he is growing up compacted into half a dozen words. But when something important happens, the story switches to dialogue. And the dialogue as I looked at it in this new project of mine often turns out to be remarkably novelistic. That is, what the characters say as they exchange words is revelatory of who they are, sometimes of their position in society, of their relationship to their interlocutor, of their psychology. And there's nothing quite like it outside the Hebrew Bible in ancient literature. Homer has great speeches, but they are speeches, not dialogue. So, I would say that the abiding interest of the Hebrew writers to which the Job poet is an exception is not in nature but in how language is used and how language shapes human reality.

AUDIENCE MEMBER: I connected to the fact that Adam had to name the animals and the language is what mattered.

AUDIENCE MEMBER: I was reading your Genesis translation, and since you have spoken about Genesis a number of times, can you explain how you came up with the first verse? You know, because I always have this parallel with the Gospel of John, "In the beginning," and you started out, "When God began to create," you know, I found that fascinating. Can you tell me how you kind of came to that?

ROBERT ALTER: First, especially after the plagiarism disaster with the recent president of Harvard University, I want to give full credit to sources. So, at least for two generations, biblical scholars in general have understood that those first three Hebrew words, *bereshit bara Elohim,* don't mean "In the beginning God created," but rather "When God began to create." That's not a new insight. Rashi, the great Hebrew commentator who lived in twelfth-century France, came to the same conclusion. Now, let me tell you why that conclusion is inevitable. It is not just because other ancient Near Eastern creation narratives, which the scholars cite, begin with a formula like "when so-and-so created" with a "when" clause. The first word is *reshit,* which means "beginning." But it's not "in the beginning," *barishit.* It's *bereshit.* I'll explain this. There is no way in Biblical Hebrew to say "the beginning," *hareshit. Reshit* is always attached to the noun or verbal noun that immediately follows in what's called the construct form. I know you studied Hebrew, so you will know what this is. In Hebrew the form is called *smikhut,* which means "attachment." As, for example, you would say in Biblical Hebrew, "in the beginning of the kingship of Jehoiakim," "*bereishit mamlekhet Yehoyakim.*" The word could not possibly mean *bareshit,* "in the beginning," because there's no *bareshit* in Biblical Hebrew. And the second word at the beginning of the Hebrew text, *bara,* which looks like a conjugated verb, either serves despite its vocalization as an infinitive, or maybe the Masoretic vocalization is wrong, and it should be the infinitive *bero,* "to begin." It's an infinitive, then, that serves as a verbal noun, literally, "in the beginning of the creating of God," which is obviously too cumbersome in English. So I translated it as "When God began to create," but, as I said, that translation is not original.

AUDIENCE MEMBER: And if I could follow up with that. When you translate, are you translating by book or are you thinking canonically in any sense? With the church fathers, of course, they find all these connections throughout the Old Testament with just a single word kind of thing. So you hear "In the beginning" in Genesis and then John starts out "In the beginning." You kind of miss that connection when you get that kind of translation. So is it by the kind of book like Genesis, one style Exodus, another style kind of thing?

ROBERT ALTER: First, the notion that the Bible is one book is shared by Christians and Jews. That is, on the Jewish side, the Midrash assumed that it was one book with multiple interconnections to all its parts. So reading a verse in Genesis could immediately lead the Midrash to a verse in Job or a verse in Psalms. I don't share that assumption at all. Now, stylistically, the first four of the Five Books of Moses are drawn from the same three principal sources. Thus there is no particular stylistic distinction among those four books. There is definitely a distinction between the priestly style, P, on the one hand and E and J on the other. (The scholarly labels with letters derive from the following: P is obviously from "priestly"; E and J are used because one source favors Elohim for the designation of the deity and the other Yahweh, which in German transliteration—the hypothesis about sources originated with the Germans—is Jahweh.) As for the Priestly writer, when he is not cataloging clean and unclean animals, tabernacle trappings, or ritual practices, when he's telling his story, he has a grand epic style with cadenced prose and balanced periodic sentences, which is quite different from E and J. As for E and J, it's a little hard to distinguish stylistically between the two, despite certain differences in terminology. To the best of my ability, I tried to get across the stylistic differences between sources in my translation. Now, when you get to Deuteronomy, the language sounds very different. Remember, it is presented as a series of Moses's valedictory addresses before his death. And the style is oratorical with long rolling sentences that are often periodic, an emphatic use of repetition, and other features associated with oratorical style. I aimed to convey that in my translation. Later Biblical Hebrew, I should add, written during and after the Babylonian exile, sounds very different again.

AUDIENCE MEMBER: Thanks. What are your thoughts on the Septuagint? Do you have much interaction with that? And do you think there's anything perhaps lost in translation going from Hebrew to Greek with poetry?

ROBERT ALTER: The Septuagint is more literal than we would allow our translations to be today. There's a big question of the textual divergences. It was using Hebrew texts that were often not word-for-word identical with the texts we have in the Masoretic texts. It also occasionally introduced whole passages which probably were not part of the original. But from time to time, you can see that they had a Hebrew text from which they were translating that sounded more reliable than the received text. It solved certain problems, and suddenly an incoherence became coherent and so forth. As to poetry, the Septuagint does little to preserve the poetic features of the Hebrew.

AUDIENCE MEMBER: Just a little comment. Your translation of the beginning of Genesis, which brings it alive in a certain way—it's interesting, there's Monsignor Knox commenting on the Vulgate translation of the prologue of John's Gospel, which is brought up here. He makes a similar comment. He says, "What can be flatter than the first verse of St. John, as usually translated, 'In the beginning was the Word,'" and so on. He said, "It suppresses a chiasmus in the way it's normally translated." And so he suggests rather than destroy the chiasmus you must have something like "God had the word abiding with him, and the Word was God." Sometimes it requires a new pair of eyes and a translator to see something as elementary as something like chiasmus, which you often notice right away, but don't because you're so used to hearing it. Just that comment.

Robert Alter: That's interesting. Thank you.

Audience member: The Jewish poet Hayyim Nahman Bialik (and other devotional commentators) mentions that "reading the scriptures in translation is like kissing your wife through a handkerchief."

Robert Alter: And that's an old trope, by the way.

Audience member: Yes, yes. And he goes on to say that he encourages us all to read the scriptures in their original language because, in a sense, we can analyze the differences of all the poetical features and the structures that you've done so brilliantly today. But at the heart of it, you know, it's God revealing his word to us. And it's manifesting in language something of this ineffable, mysterious essence. And so this might be an unfair question, but I just wanted to know, as someone who has spent so much time with how God has revealed Himself to His chosen people in the past, what it taught you about who God is and what do you take away from how he expressed himself in this language?

ROBERT ALTER: Well, I would say you have to come away with a sense that God is more complicated than we think He is, and the understanding of who God is evolves, certainly through the books of the Hebrew Bible. The New Testament is a little bit different because all those books were composed within a few decades of each other. By contrast, the Hebrew Bible comprises texts written over many centuries. The oldest of them, like the Song of Deborah, go back to around 1100 B.C.E. or not long after. And the most recent, the Book of Daniel, is around 165. So that's almost nine hundred years. God in the Garden story, in the J source, which is the oldest, is imagined in frankly anthropomorphic terms. And maybe at that point in time, when the J writer was fashioning his story, people couldn't imagine God differently. He's imagined, as I've noted, in very anthropomorphic terms. That is, He goes for a walk in the cool of the evening, when the sun has begun to set and the hot, Middle Eastern day has passed, and a person can go out for a walk again. Nothing like that happens when we turn to Exodus. We all tend as Christians and Jews to think of God through the prism of later theology. So, let's say you might think of God in Aristotelian terms via Thomas Aquinas. Or if you're a Jew, you would do the same thing through Maimonides. But as you go from book to book in the Hebrew Bible, you see the approaches to God and understandings of God changed over time, or maybe even in the same time different believers had different takes on God. Now let me add one thing which goes back to my translation. I've been emphasizing how important the literary crafting of the texts is for their meaning, for what we call their message. I would amplify this by saying that my effort to convey the literary shaping of the Hebrew by no means pushes to the back burner my concern for getting the exact meaning precise. One example of this concern for precision that was not at all original with me was "When God began to create," but here's a rather different example. You all know the creation story and the garden story with Adam as its protagonist. In the Hebrew, however, there is no "Adam." Okay, I know this might upset some people, but the explanation is very simple. Adam, later, as far as I know, not in the biblical period, becomes a Hebrew name. And of course, it's an English name. We all know people who have been named Adam. But in the Garden story, he's always referred to as *ha'adam*, "the *adam*." You almost never put a definite article before a name. You don't say "the Charlie." Well, you could satirically, as in the coinage, "the Donald," but I won't go into that. So there is the memorable verse we know by heart. "In the image of God He created man," except it doesn't say "man." It says "the *adam*." It can't really mean "Adam." It means "the human." And we know that it's not differentiated according to gender, even though grammatically it's masculine in the Hebrew, because the second half of the verse is "male and female, He created them." So I was stuck with a quandary. How do you translate an ordinary term like "the *adam*"? And I decided I would be betraying the precise meaning of the Hebrew, which I cared about a lot, by translating it as "Adam" or as "man." In consequence, I did this slightly weird thing. Sometimes you have to make compromises as a translator. I translated it as "the human." The disadvantage of that is that it sounds a little bit like something out of a science fiction narrative. You know, the aliens come out of their spaceship and seeing a person, say, "There's the human standing there!" But I thought it was being honest in regard to what the Hebrew says. I did strive mightily to get at the exact meaning though sometimes you can't. Sometimes it's guesswork. Now we all know that nuance is important in language. That is, there's a difference, for example, between a crook and a criminal. A crook is more insulting (synonyms are never entirely identical in meaning). You could have a sentence such as "He has now been declared by a New York court a criminal, even though I always thought he was an honest man." But if you say, "He was a crook," you're emphatically hitting him with a denigrating label, not just a legal judgment. Let me give you one biblical example of a nuance of difference between ostensible synonyms. Most of you probably remember the terrible story of Amnon and Tamar, in which Amnon, pretending to be ill, lures Tamar to his bedchamber in order to rape her. He asks their shared father—she's his half-sister—to send him Tamar to bring him food. Except that there are two normal words for food in Biblical Hebrew. One is *okhel* from the verb that means "to eat." And the other is *leḥem*, "bread," which is a synecdoche for all kinds of food. But neither is the word that is used here. It is a rather rare word, *biryah*, which I double-checked in a concordance, my greatest guide in translating, a Hebrew concordance to the Bible. Every time *biryah* is used, it's used in an instance where the person being fed has been doing poorly, as Amnon pretends is the case for him, or has been fasting. So it isn't ordinary food. It's like chicken soup. But I couldn't use chicken soup because they hadn't domesticated the chicken yet. In the end, I settled for "nourishment." But you see, that distinction is important for this moment in the narrative, for stressing Amnon's pretending to be ill. In this way, I did my best to convey the precise nuances of the Hebrew, but of course I was not always successful. I'm sure there are instances of poor judgment on my part or error, or whatever. No translation is perfect. But I did make every effort to get at the precise meaning and also, the nuance of connotation, of the Hebrew words.

Audience member: I know the answer to this, because I've asked you before.

Robert Alter: I may have a different answer.

Audience member: Which could make it even more fun! When you started to translate Genesis, did you intend to do the whole thing?

Robert Alter: Oh, no. Not at all. For various reasons, after a conversation with a publisher in New York, I decided to try to translate the Book of Genesis. That's all I had in mind. And I still have this visual image of looking at the first page in Hebrew and thinking, am I really going to do this? And from the get-go, I had this idea, because the stylistic values as I've been arguing in both these lectures are so important to me, of trying to get something that was close to the stylistic effects of the Hebrew. But a little voice in my head said, "This is not doable." Because the two languages are different in structure. They're different in syntax, and many of the key terms barely overlap in meaning. So, I said to myself, I will try to do this, and it will look silly, and everybody will hate it, and maybe I will hate it too. But, somehow or other, it turned out to be a much better approximation of what I wanted to do than I thought I could come up with. And it was very well received, so I said, "OK, I'll do one more book of the Bible," and since after the story of Joseph and his brothers, the other most remarkable biblical narrative, which seems to me to be an amazingly great narrative, is the David story, I decided to do that, which is basically 1 and 2 Samuel. And then I translated Psalms. From there I went on to the Five

Books of Moses. And I was just having fun with it while, I should say, I also continued to pursue my interests in modern literature. So I wasn't working nonstop at this. That helped keep me sane. And then, about maybe six or seven years ago, I looked at what I had actually published. It was two-thirds of the whole Hebrew Bible. So I realized that if I could get through the prophets, books that are both a linguistic and a philological challenge, I could do the whole Hebrew Bible. And that is what I did.

AUDIENCE MEMBER: Did this come out of the books that you had written on biblical narrative and biblical poetry that you knew the translations weren't up to snuff? Is that why the editor thought you ought to do it? Or you thought you ought to do it?

AUDIENCE MEMBER: Not exactly.

AUDIENCE MEMBER: We are all glad you did, by the way.

ROBERT ALTER: When I wrote the book on biblical narrative, I wasn't at all thinking of how to translate the Bible, and so while I did ad hoc translations of passages to analyze, I had no notion of how to do it. And at the time I more or less followed the path marked out by the modern translations by committee, especially the one done by the Jewish Publication Society. I assumed these are serious, well-trained biblical scholars, so what they do in translation must be the right way. But a new perception came to me about translating the Bible about fourteen years ago. The publisher of my books on biblical narrative and biblical poetry asked me to do revised editions. In the course of revising I did make some small changes in the body of my texts and provided a few amplifications of what I had originally written. When, however, I looked at the translations I had done in the 1980s, I was horrified and said to myself, "Those are awful!" I proceeded to substitute for all those translations I had done for the initial publication of the narrative and poetry books either the new translations from biblical books I'd already published, or if the passages were from biblical books I had not yet translated, I made new translations for the revised editions. Through this process, I became vividly aware of what was wrong with the existing translations of the Bible that had influenced me early on.

AUDIENCE MEMBER: I was hoping you could explain why you said that Isaiah 11 doesn't have any eschatological intention behind it, especially since you also said that it is the common Christian and Jewish interpretation. Do we have any reason for not?

ROBERT ALTER: Yes, because I think that the prophets were thinking politically and historically. And so I am convinced actual history was what Isaiah had in mind—I can't say this with absolute certainty, I don't want to be presumptuous—but I think what he envisioned was an ideal ruler who would appear at some future moment, somebody who would be like Abraham Lincoln and George Washington all rolled in one, a royal figure who would make the kingdom of Judah an entirely just and decent country and somehow restore peace in the land. But his use of poetic hyperbole, a recurrent feature of prophetic poetry, pushed the language in the direction that would become eschatological. That's my understanding of it, though I would grant the possibility that Isaiah son of Amoz really imagined a totally transformative end of history when everything would radically change. I think that's a possible reading, so I don't want to say that anybody who reads it that way is dead wrong. To me, however, it seems a less plausible reading. That is, I don't really think that Isaiah in the 620s, or whenever it was that he was prophesying, literally believed that there was going to come a time when a lion would lie down with a lamb, and when infants would play unharmed at the den of vipers. That seems to me to have been a belief that was outside his system of assumptions about reality because he was so concerned with the present state of society in the real world. That is my understanding of this and related passages that have been read eschatologically, but I don't want to claim that I'm absolutely sure.

AUDIENCE MEMBER: Thank you for these presentations. It brings me back to my studies in modern Hebrew and Biblical Hebrew. You know, so often as a pastor or clergy, you're looking at the text, even just as a believer, you're asking the audience, "What's the intent"? And what's the principle we want to take out of it? But we fail to marinate, kind of, in the beauty of the text. So, what would be your advice, if you could speak to a president of a seminary and say, "Look. This is what you ought to include to help people just appreciate the value of settling into, rather than rushing through, the exegesis, just to get the point I've got to give to the people."

ROBERT ALTER: I think that that's what I tried to do with my commentary on the Hebrew Bible. The commentary was another thing I didn't intend to do originally. Many good things occur, at least in my experience, by happenstance. And an important happenstance for me was writing a commentary. That is, as I've said, I didn't intend it at first. What I thought I would do was from time to time provide a translator's note, such as: this is an obscure word, the meaning is uncertain, or, there is a significant pun in the original that can't be translated. But by the time I got halfway through the first chapter of Genesis I discovered there were all kinds of things going on in the text that I wanted to talk about, things that the traditional scholarly translators and commentators did not address because they had no literary perspective. I should add that my commentary isn't entirely restricted to a literary perspective because for readers today, you have to explain certain things about ancient Israelite law and marriage and divorce, about property law, and so on that are totally unfamiliar to us, and it was also important to note, as scholars have done, where there are influences from Babylonian or Egyptian literature and from Canaanite mythology. In any case, much of my commentary is focused on the aspects in the literary fashioning of the Hebrew that make the text come alive —in its vivid and revelatory dialogue, its representation of subtle turns of psychology, its shifts in linguistic register, its deployment of literary allusion. To the best of my ability, that's what I tried to do.

AUDIENCE MEMBER: Is there any other poetry you would recommend people read if you were teaching them how to do this, aside from the Bible, that's maybe more accessible?

ROBERT ALTER: Oh, you mean poetry outside the Bible?

AUDIENCE MEMBER: Yes.

ROBERT ALTER: I guess I would not recommend Milton, who's a great poet, and who of course took up the biblical story in *Paradise Lost* (and also in *Samson Agonistes*). His poetry, however, is entirely unlike biblical poetry.

AUDIENCE MEMBER: T. S. Eliot?

ROBERT ALTER: T. S. Eliot, yes, at least in some respects. More so, Gerard Manley Hopkins, who was a Catholic poet in a monastic order. And for biblical poetry, I would also recommend a few poets who cultivated plain language such William Carlos Williams and Seamus Heaney. Though biblical poetry is formally quite different from English poetry, there are some poets you can learn from in this regard.

2
JOB

The writer responsible for Job is the greatest of all biblical poets and one of the most remarkable poets who flourished in any language in the ancient Mediterranean world. He is a technical virtuoso, deftly marshaling sound and rhythm for expressive effects, at times deploying brilliant wordplay—as when he writes, "My days are swifter than a weaver's shuttle, / they snap off without any hope" (7:6), the word for "hope," *tiqwah*, punning on a homonym that means "thread." He utilizes a vocabulary that is the biggest of any biblical poet, with borrowings from Aramaic, enlisting rare words and even introducing words that seem to be his own invention. His range of metaphors is inventive and often dazzling, drawing on cheese making, weaving, horticulture, and much more. Had there been bicycles in ancient Israel, I suspect we would find a bicycle simile somewhere in his poem. He exhibits an interest in nature quite untypical of biblical poets. And no other poet of his time and place possessed his ability to link together different passages with recurrent terms and images, even over long stretches of text. We know nothing about this anonymous heterodox genius except that he probably lived in the fifth century B.C.E., and even that has been disputed.

In the fluidity of forms that characterized the late biblical period, it would certainly have been possible for him to frame his argument in prose, but poetry was an inevitable choice for him. The power of poetic expression gave him the means to articulate the full measure of Job's anguish and his outrage at having been severely mistreated by God, while also conveying the dizzying span of God's vision of the created world in the Voice from the Whirlwind at the end. He surely knew that he had a mastery of the poetic medium, and he relished its deployment in the great work he produced. The outlook of the Job poet is a radical dissent from the mainstream biblical consensus, and in this regard, too, poetry was a powerful vehicle for him to express that dissent. In what follows, I will be examining two rather long passages, the first a complete poem, in order to show how the resources of poetry enabled him to say what he wanted to say.

He strategically frames his poetic argument by beginning with a searing death-wish poem that communicates Job's acute sense that his existence has become so unbearable—all his children dead, his flocks destroyed, his body afflicted with an excruciating burning rash—that he wishes he never would have been born. Here is the poem that takes up all of chapter 3.

> Annul the day that I was born
>   and the night that said, "A man is conceived."
> That day, let it be darkness.
>   Let God above not seek it out,
>   nor brightness shine upon it.
> Let darkness, death's shadow, foul it,
>   let a cloud-mass rest upon it,

let day-gloom dismay it.
That night, let murk overtake it.
　　Let it not join in the days of the year,
　　　　let it not enter the number of months.
Oh, let that night be barren,
　　let it have no song of joy.
Let the day-cursers hex it,
　　those ready to rouse Leviathan.
Let its twilight stars go dark.
　　Let it hope for day in vain,
　　　　and let it not see the eyelids of dawn.
For it did not shut the belly's doors
　　to hide wretchedness from my eyes.
Why did I not die from the womb,
　　from the belly come out, breathe my last?
Why did knees welcome me,
　　and why breasts, that I should suck?
For now I would lie and be still,
　　would sleep and know repose
with kings and the councilors of earth,
　　who build ruins for themselves,
or with princes, possessors of gold,
　　who fill their houses with silver.
Or like a buried stillborn I'd be,
　　like babes who never saw light.
There the wicked cease their troubling,
　　and there the weary repose.
All together the prisoners are tranquil,
　　they hear not the taskmaster's voice.
The small and the great are there,
　　and the slave is free of his master.
Why give light to the wretched
　　and life to the deeply embittered,

> who wait for death in vain,
>> dig for it more than for treasure,
> who rejoice at the tomb,
>> are glad when they find the grave?
> —To a man whose way is hidden,
>> and God has hedged him about.
> For before my bread my moaning comes,
>> and my roar pours out like water.
> For I feared a thing—it befell me,
>> what I dreaded came upon me.
> I was not quiet, I was not still,
>> I had no repose, and trouble came. (3:3–26)

The first word of the poem, *yo 'vad,* literally means "perish," but unfortunately "perish the day" is no longer a viable English equivalent because the locution in our era has slid into prissiness ("perish the thought"). The effort of a couple of modern translators to give the expression punch in English ("damn the day") inserts an inappropriate tone or implication because there is nothing about damning, in either the invective or the theological sense, in the Hebrew. The transitive verb "annul" has the justification that the poem is all about expunging the day from the calendar. The two versets of this line exhibit an altogether original use of the dynamic of intensification from the first verset to the second that we tracked in Isaiah. Job wishes not merely never to have been born but, moving back nine months, never to have been conceived. Thus the conventional poetic word-pair, "day" and then "night," is given a startling new force. The poet then picks up "night" from the second half of this line and launches on a rich orchestration of synonyms for darkness. After the primary term "darkness," he enlists "cloud-mass," "day-gloom," "murk." ("Day-gloom," *kimrirei yom*, seems to be his coinage, probably derived from an Aramaic root that indicates darkness, with the expression here possibly referring to a solar eclipse.) The poet's tapping of the Hebrew lexicon for synonyms is evident throughout the book. (There are five different terms for *lion* in Biblical Hebrew, and at one point he uses all five in two consecutive lines.) With elegant appropriateness, Job in this poem wants the night of his conception to have been "barren," which is of course the opposite of conception.

In the process of intensification as the poem continues, he then moves up to a mythological register: "Let the day-cursers hex it, / those ready to rouse Leviathan." A minor emendation to the Masoretic text yields *Yamm*, the primordial sea-god who is also Leviathan, instead of *yom,* "day." (At this point, the King James Version commits one of its most lamentable errors, rendering the Hebrew for Leviathan, *lewayatan,* as "their mourning," which is both grammatically wrong and imagines the noun is *lewayah,* a term for "funeral" in rabbinic Hebrew that is not biblical.) The second line in this verse makes the wish for darkness cosmic, still another aspect of intensification—no stars, a night without dawn, without morning stars. The concluding metaphor of this line demonstrates how utterly original the Job poet is in his deployment of figurative language: "let it not see the eyelids of dawn." This is a daring, and beautiful, metaphor: the first crack of light on the eastern horizon is likened to the opening eyelids of the sleeper looking out to the east. Modern translators, deluded in thinking that readers can no longer understand metaphors, substitute for the metaphor what may be its referent, as in the Jewish Publication Society's "the glimmerings of the dawn." The Job poet knew that this was a remarkable metaphor, for he did not hesitate to use it again much later in a radically different context, in representing the fierce appearance of the daunting Leviathan, thus locating beauty at the heart of terror: "His sneezes shoot out light, / and his eyes are like the eyelids of the dawn" (41:10).

The initial movement of the death-wish poem heads toward a conclusion by Job's saying of the day he was born that it "did not shut the belly's doors / to hide wretchedness from my eyes." The prominent noun in the last phrase is a strong instance of poetic efficiency. We might expect here "life" or "the light," but for this sufferer life itself has become nothing but wretchedness. In the next few lines, following the characteristic movement of biblical poetry from the general to the specific or concrete, we get an evocation of the physicality of birth: womb, belly, knees (presumably parted in birthing), and breasts giving suck.

At verse 14, Job's wish never to have been born joins with a panorama of human life, and it is a bleak panorama. Kings "build ruins for themselves," imposing structures that inevitably crumble to dust (one thinks of Shelley's "Ozymandius"), and princes store up gold and silver, futilely, for they will part from it in death. Verse 16 shows the poet's firm sense of integrated structure, of which we will see a more spectacular instance in the Voice from the Whirlwind, for "babes who never saw light" takes us back to the early lines expressing the wish to be a stillborn and blot out the light. Everyone, in this despairing vision, finds repose only in death, the great equalizer. And what has life been for humankind? The wicked have troubled others, all are weary, there are prisoners and slaves and taskmasters. Existence is so universally miserable that everyone longs for death. In this way Job invites us to see his wretchedness not as a special case but merely as a particular instance of the fate of misery shared by all. The large resonance of Job's inveighing against God as he proceeds in his poetic argument derives from his seeing unwarranted suffering not as his alone but as the common plight of humankind.

A single word toward the end of this poem exemplifies how this writer creates connective links in the overall structure of his work. In the frame-story, the Adversary says to God, "Have you not hedged him about and his household and all that he has all around?" (1:10). The verb here obviously has the sense of "protected." But the same word in Job's mouth here, "and God has hedged him about" means the opposite: Job is complaining that God has blocked him on all sides, left him no way out of his terrible plight. This sharp play on two opposed meanings of the same word might suggest that the Job poet did not transcribe the old folktale verbatim that had come down to him, probably orally, but felt free at least at one point and perhaps others to modify a wording. Alternately, the folktale may have included "hedge," which the poet then played against. That same verb will occur twice more in the Voice from the Whirlwind, with still a third meaning, but I will postpone commenting on its use there until we have a long look at the God speech that concludes the poetic body of the book.

The final lines of the death-wish poem aptly round off its argument. The third line before the end exhibits the expected biblical intensification from verset to verset: "For before my bread my moaning comes, / and my roar pours out like water," from moaning to roaring. Job goes on to assert that he had lived in a state of anxiety, perhaps intimated in his offering sacrifices for his children because he was afraid they had committed some offense; and, finally, having longed for the quiet of the grave, he admits the realization of those fears. The last word of the Hebrew text is *rogez,* etymologically, a state of disturbance or unrest, as this same verbal stem is used elsewhere to describe the shaking of earthquakes.

The devastating extremity of Job's wish for nonbeing raises a general issue. It serves the obvious purpose of introducing all that he will say by making clear how utterly unbearable his suffering is. He does not yet indict God, but that will follow, for he never ceases to believe in an all-powerful God, which means that God must be responsible for the chain of disasters inflicted upon him. But what good can poetry do in the face of intolerable and unwarranted suffering? The Job poet is clearly not alone in confronting this dilemma. In English literature, perhaps the most memorable instance is Lear driven out on the moor in the fierce storm, blinded, stripped of his possessions, cruelly rejected by two of his three daughters: "I am bound / Upon a wheel of fire, that mine own tears / Do scald like molten lead." The Job poet would have appreciated this figurative language, especially the way the wheel of fire is extended in the simile of the scalding tears like molten lead. In our own time, the signal instance of poetry conveying unbearable suffering may well be Paul Celan's celebrated *Todesfuge* ("Death Fugue"). It is a formally deft, beautifully crafted poem, but it embodies "a terrible beauty," in Yeats's phrase. The first two words, then repeated as a kind of refrain, are a shock: "black milk." The violent transformation of the nurturing substance of life into blackness will then work in tandem with another refrain-phrase, "Death is a master from Deutschland." Celan exploits the resources of poetry to express the unspeakable outrage of six million of his people murdered in the industrial death-machine of Deutschland, the cherished homeland figured in the poem by the fair Margarete. What, in confronting such appalling realities, can poetry possibly do? The reflexive response to outrage against our moral instincts is, I suppose, a scream. Poetry of this order of greatness, from Job to Celan, transforms the scream into articulated, eloquent expression. I don't think it's really cathartic, but it communicates a feeling that suffering has been endowed with a sharp focus in language, the primary human medium, that outrage has been given a voice, a voice that gets across the full awfulness of what has occurred and therefore is, in a weird way at once horrifying and satisfying—we somehow cling to our humanity in the face of horror.

As the great poem of Job unfolds, it emerges that it incorporates three different orders of poetry. Most prominent, until a new poetic voice appears at the end, is Job's poetry. The poetry of the three comforters in the debate is by and large inferior to his. It is inferior because they are working with the complacent clichés of traditional wisdom and so the poetry they speak in their argument invokes many shopworn formulas. From time to time there are brief passages of strong poetry because this writer was such a fine poet that he could scarcely refrain from intermittently giving the comforters a few good lines. Finally, when we come to the conclusion of the poetic body of the work, the poet takes a certain risk, at which he succeeds splendidly. God is now, at last, speaking, and because He is God, He must be given poetry that transcends the stunning poetry of anguish spoken by Job. It is a challenge that the Job poet undertakes because he must have been confident in his own mastery. If I may propose a seemingly irreverent analogy, let me cite Molly Bloom's soliloquy that is the concluding episode of James Joyce's *Ulysses*. She has been a looming presence in the novel, especially in her husband's thoughts, as we are taken through a rich variety of remarkable prose poetry, some of it stream of consciousness and some of it in other forms. Then, at the end, we enter the living current of her unspoken words as she lies in bed, mulling over the day, her husband, her loves, her life, and this soliloquy proves to be prose poetry arguably even greater than all that has come before. Like the Voice from the Whirlwind, it is poetic language that embodies a grand epiphany, the resonant affirmation that the work as a whole is meant to pronounce. Something analogous occurs in the Voice from the Whirlwind.

God's poem begins with a challenge to Job: "Who is this who darkens counsel / in words without knowledge?" (38:2). The initial phrase demonstrates how aptly this poet chooses his words. "Darken counsel" is not an idiom that appears elsewhere in the Bible, and so it evidently has been coined for the present purpose. Job's first poem, as we saw, begins with a whole sequence of images that express a longing to blot out the light—daylight, the rising sun, the stars, all things to be engulfed by darkness. In response, God signals in the very phrasing that this is profoundly misguided. After a line in which He tells Job to gird his loins like a man, God continues:

> Where were you when I founded earth?
>   Tell, if you know understanding.
> Who fixed its measures, do you know,
>   or who stretched a line upon it?
> In what were its sockets sunk,
>   or who laid its cornerstone,
> when the morning stars sang together,
>   and all the sons of God shouted for joy?
> Who hedged the sea with double doors,
>   when it gushed forth from the womb,
> when I made clouds its clothing,
>   and thick mists its swaddling bands?
> I made breakers upon it My limit,
>   and set a bolt with double doors.
> And I said, "Thus far come, no farther,
>   here halt the surge of your waves."
> Have you ever commanded the morning,
>   appointed the dawn to its place,
> to seize the earth's corners,
>   that the wicked be shaken from it?
> It turns like sealing clay,
>   takes color like a garment,
> and their light is withdrawn from the wicked,
>   and the upraised arm is broken.

Have you ever come into the springs of the sea,
  in the bottommost deep walked about?
Have the gates of death been laid bare to you,
  and the gates of death's shadow have you seen?
Did you take in the breadth of the earth?
 Tell, if you know it all.
Where is the way that light dwells,
  and darkness, where is its place,
that you might take it to its home
  and understand the paths to its house?
You know, for you were born then,
  and the number of your days is great!
Have you come into the storehouse of snow,
  the storehouse of hail have you seen,
which I keep for a time of strife,
  for a day of battle and war?
By what way does the west wind fan out,
  the east wind whip over the earth?
Who split a channel for the torrent,
  and a way for the thunderstorm,
to rain on a land without man,
  wilderness bare of humankind,
to sate the desolate dunes,
  and make the grass sprout there?
Does the rain have a father,
  or who begot the drops of dew?
From whose belly did the ice come forth,
  to the frost of the heavens who gave birth?
Water congeals like stone,

and the face of the deep locks hard. (38:4–30)

The arresting image of the morning stars singing together in joy singles out these points of light in the night sky, heralding a dawn that Job wished had never come. There are more references to light further on. This is an imagining of creation not hinted at in Genesis, though we do not know whether it is the poet's original invention or whether it reflects a tradition about creation on which he drew but that was left out of Genesis. In the next line, we get the sea "hedged" with double doors. That verb, we recall, occurred in two different senses in the frame-story and in the death-wish poem. Now, the idea it conveys in this moment of cosmogony is a blocking of the surging waters of the sea from flooding the land. That notion is inherited from Canaanite poetry, where it is accompanied by the mythological motif of the conquest and imprisonment of a monstrous sea-god, variously called Yamm, Leviathan, Rahab, Tanin (the last also refers to lesser sea-beasts), effected by the land-god (or weather-god) Baal. This old story was so familiar in the culture that Job could invoke it without explanation to signify God's holding him captive under relentless surveillance: "Am I Yamm, or the Sea-Beast [*tanin*], / that You should put a watch upon me?" (7:12). The explicitly mythological figure is excluded from the representation here. Instead, we witness the waters gushing forth from the "womb" of the primordial sea, an image for it invented by the Job poet. This strategically chosen metaphor thus represents creation as birth, the very thing Job wanted to cancel in his death wish. Birth is confirmed in the following line: "when I made clouds its clothing, / and thick mists its swaddling bands." This is a metaphorical coinage of the same level of originality as Shakespeare's scalding tears of molten lead. In the ancient world, infants were wrapped snugly in swaddling bands, strips of white linen. These are like what one might see looking out to the west at bands of mist over the water. The strikingly visual image is completely unusual while it continues the figuration of creation as birth.

Verses 17–20 further develop the rejoinder to Job's initial poem bleak poem: "Have the gates of death been laid before you, / and the gates of death's shadow have you seen?" Job had fervently wished for death but knew nothing of its looming reality. God alone is the master of death, His all-seeing eyes taking in the full measure of its dark realm. The next two verses underscore the antithesis to chapter 3:

> Where is the way that light dwells,
>   and darkness, where is its place,
> that you might take it to its home
>   and understand the paths to its house? (38:19-20)

Light appears here in the poetic parallelism with darkness, as it does elsewhere in the Bible, but that appearance is diametrically opposed to Job's desire for light to be swallowed up by darkness. Instead, there is a diurnal rhythm of alternation between light and darkness—and just possibly, by implication, between hope and despair. Light and darkness are part of the harmonious ongoing process of the created world, something the devastated Job has chosen to turn away from.

What follows in the poem is a manifestation of the powerful, at times even violent, energy that pulses through creation, a theme that will continue through this poem all the way down to Behemoth and Leviathan at the end. This might be the relevance at this point in the mythological reference to God's setting aside the harsh elements as weapons "for a time of strife, / for a day of battle and war." The face of nature itself is limned with violent action—"Who split a channel for the torrent, / and a way for the thunderstorm."

At this juncture, the poet introduces a crucial, and radical, idea: God brings "rain on a land without man, / wilderness bare of humankind, // to sate the desolate dunes, / and make the grass sprout there." The version of cosmogony in Genesis is emphatically anthropocentric. Humankind is the culmination of creation, enjoined to rule over all things, everything set out for his benefit. Here, by contrast, God causes the rain to fall "on a land without man," a rainfall that will "sate the desolate dunes." (The poet's mastery of sound as well as metaphor is evident in these words: "desolate dunes" represents the Hebrew *sho'ah umesho'ah*, that alliteration merely approximated in my English phrase.) This dissenting notion that the natural world extends far beyond humankind and is perhaps indifferent to him surely resonated with Melville in *Moby-Dick,* perhaps as much as Job's Leviathan, which the novelist chose to construe as a great whale.

Finally, in the next lines, the poem returns to the birth imagery prominent at the beginning:

> Does the rain have a father,
>   or who begot the drops of dew?
> From whose belly did the ice come forth,
>   to the frost of the heavens who gave birth?
> (38:28-29)

The second line here demonstrates both the originality and the boldness of this poet in his handling of metaphor. Having chosen to figure the origins of ice and dew as a birth, he represents that birth in a way that is almost shocking when he invites us to contemplate chunks of ice emerging from the womb. Poetry can be a means of reorienting or radically shifting perception, especially in conjoining through figurative language totally disparate and surprising ideas or realms. This is clearly what God wants to do with Job—to shake him up, to compel him to see the world in ways that would never have occurred to him.

After leading Job's vision to the sky in the next few lines, the Voice from the Whirlwind moves on at the end of the chapter to the animal kingdom, with particular attention to beasts of prey—the lion and the raven. (One should remember that chapter divisions in the Bible were a medieval editorial intervention, and the lines I am referring to were meant to initiate the tour of zoology that will continue to the end of the poem.) This zoological section, running to the end of chapter 39, then picking up after a few lines of address by God to Job with the climactic Behemoth and Leviathan in chapters 40 and 41, is too long for a reading here, but we can look at two passages. The first is in chapter 39:

> Do you know the mountain goats' birth time,
>   do you mark the calving of the gazelles?
> Do you number the months till they come to term
>   and know their birthing time?
> They crouch, burst forth with their babes,
>   their young they push out to the world.
> Their offspring batten, grow big in the wild,
>   they go out and do not return.
> Who set the wild ass free,
>   and the onager's reins who loosed,
> whose home I made in the steppes,
>   his dwelling place flats of salt?
> He scoffs at the bustling city,
>   the driver's shouts he does not hear.

> He roams mountains for his forage,
>   and every green thing he seeks.
> Will the wild ox want to serve you,
>   pass the night at your feeding trough?
> Bind the wild ox with cord for the furrow,
>   will he harrow the valleys behind you?
> Can you rely on him with his great power
>   and leave your labor to him?
> Can you trust him to bring back seed,
>   gather grain on your threshing floor? (39:1–12)

We are now returned to the theme of birth announced in the figurative language at the beginning of the poem. Birth is universal among animate creatures, and it goes on, far from human observation or human ken, in the mountains and the forests, beyond the grasp of the man who wished for his own birth never to have occurred. The animals of the wild "burst forth" with their little ones. Even birth, paradoxically, is imagined as a violent process. This is a unique application of this verb to birthing—the general meaning of the verbal stem is "to split apart"—an indication that the poet is imagining procreation in a different way. The lines that follow take up a theme that will become more salient in the representation of Behemoth and Leviathan. The wild ass and the onager, out on the salt flats and the steppes, live remote from any human control, scoffing at the crowded habitations of men and women, free from the whips and the commands of the driver.

As one sees elsewhere in biblical poetry, intensification within the single line is projected forward through a sequence of lines. In the four lines devoted to the wild ox, the poem's audience is challenged with the question of whether they can ever domesticate the wild ass and subject him to servitude, hitch him to the plow, train him (fantastically) to bring back seed or gather grain from the threshing floor. This theme of the resistance of the beast to human mastery will be elevated to a new level of intensity in Behemoth and Leviathan. All this is a strong expression of the rejection of anthropocentrism: contrary to the assurances of Genesis 1, humankind will never be able to rule over the animal kingdom. There are forms of life simply too powerful for man. A few lines down, the poem goes on:

> Do you give might to the horse,
>   do you clothe his neck with a mane?
> Do you make him roar like locusts—
>   his splendid snort is terror.
> He churns up the valley exulting,
>   in power goes out to the clash arms.
> He scoffs at fear and is undaunted,
>   turns not back before the sword.
> Over him rattles the quiver,
>   the blade, the javelin, and the spear.
> With clamor and clatter he swallows the ground,
>   and ignores the trumpet's sound.
> At the trumpet he says, "Aha,"
>   and from afar he scents the fray,
>   the thunder of captains, the shouts.
> Does the hawk soar by your wisdom,
>   spread his wings to fly away south?
> By your word does the eagle mount,
>   and set his nest on high?
> On the crag he dwells and beds down,
>   on the crest of the crag his stronghold.
> From there he seeks out food,
>   from afar his eyes look down.

> His chicks lap up blood,
> where the slain are, there he is. (39:19–30)

At this moment in the poem, before the eagle and before Behemoth and Leviathan, the poet introduces his celebrated description of the warhorse. Some readers may wonder what it is doing here. There is one plausible explanation that does not immediately justify its inclusion in the Voice from the Whirlwind. He put the warhorse in because he was drawn to do it and knew he could evoke this bellicose equine presence with remarkable vividness. He gets the sound of weaponry around the horse just right, enriching the depiction with an expressive alliteration —"clamor and clatter" in my version emulates the Hebrew *ra'ash werogez*, with the accent on the first syllable of each alliterated noun. Sound plays an energizing role in the effect of the passage —the rattle of the quiver and the weapons, the clamor of the pounding hoofbeats, the blast of the martial trumpet. With all this, the fierce battle charger prepares the way for the two daunting beasts yet to come, Behemoth and Leviathan. Like them, he is at once glorious and frightening: "his splendid snort is terror." Also like them, he embodies power and fearsome beauty that are beyond humanity, that do not relate to humankind: "Do you give might to the horse, / do you clothe his neck with a mane?" The warhorse, in contrast to the wild ass and the onager, is surely saddled with a rider holding reins, at the command of the mounted warrior. The main point is that this fearless creature galloping into the midst of battle is imagined— in this one respect, unrealistically—as though he were virtually autonomous, charging into the fray out of the sheer love of armed combat. The poet needs this divergence from verisimilitude in order to set the stage for those two creatures, Behemoth and Leviathan, who are impermeable to any human intervention.

They will make their climactic appearance, beginning in

verse 15 of the next chapter, after an intervention addressed by God to Job (40:1–14). But before that, in the last five verses of chapter 39, we move from the battlefield to the sky in the depiction of the hawk and the eagle. It is an appropriate place for the naturalistic phase of the zoological parade to end because it is a realm no human being can ever reach. Even the nests of these creatures of the sky are unreachable, placed in the crags of high mountains. But what is it the poet focuses on in the life cycle of the eagle? The eagle nurtures his young, an instinct that impels all creatures. The nurturing of the fledglings, however, necessitates killing: "His chicks lap up blood, / where the slain are, there he is." I have been contending that this writer, virtually unique in biblical poetry, is a poet keenly interested in nature, but that interest is resolutely unsentimental. There is no anthropomorphizing in his vision of the natural world, no pathetic fallacy, no gentle rhapsodizing over the beauties of creation. He understands that nature is red of tooth and claw—the eagle's chicks "lap up blood"—and that is the harsh order of things. He lucidly sees that violence, even lethal violence, is an intrinsic element of the life cycle in the animal kingdom. This does not really answer Job's complaint about unjust suffering, but it does suggest that the world around us does not conform to our comforting assumptions about good and evil and that we have to live with a reality that resists our conventional moral calculus.

I will not consider Behemoth and Leviathan directly because our scrutiny of the fierce creatures from the lion to the warhorse to the eagle anticipates much of what needs to be said about them. The difference between these two and the preceding creatures in the catalog of animals is that they straddle the border between zoology and mythology, thus culminating the poetic process of intensification. Presumably, they are based, respectively, on the hippopotamus and the crocodile, creatures of the Nile conveniently removed from the direct observation of the poet and his audience, mainly reported to them through travelers' yarns. There are realistic touches in the depiction of both, Behemoth in the shallows of the river shaded by lotus and willow, "hedged"—again that strategic verb—by the lotus; Leviathan with his crocodile's plate of armor, "His back is rows of shields, / locked close with the tightest shield," and his fearsome teeth, "All around his teeth is terror" (41:6). But such naturalistic depiction seamlessly slips into the supernatural. "Could one take him with one's eyes," it is said of Behemoth, "with barbs pierce his nose?" (40:24). though in fact the Egyptians did hunt hippopotami. Before long, the naturalistic crocodile morphs into a dragon, his mouth shooting firebrands, his nostrils emitting smoke. He is impregnable to all man's weapons (a note Melville would pick up in associating Leviathan with the Great White Whale): "When he rears up, the gods are frightened, / when he crashes down they cringe" (41:17). At this point, Leviathan has merged with the ferocious Canaanite sea-god from whom he takes his name. In the logic of the poem, the poet needs these mythologized beasts for his conclusion because they crown his argument that there are things in nature beyond human ken and absolutely beyond any hope of human domination. The psalmist, in a splendid celebration of man's supreme place in a cosmic hierarchy, wrote: "You make him rule over the work of Your hands. / All things You set under his feet." (Ps. 8:7). Tellingly, Job the sufferer quotes another line from this same psalm—"What is man that You should note him?" but bitterly reverses the meaning to say: What is miserable man that You constantly scrutinize him to persecute him? Here, in the climax of God's speech to Job, the idea that man exerts dominion over all things is powerfully opposed.

The writer responsible for this extraordinary book was not only a very bold poet—among other things coining imagery, as we have seen, that would not have occurred to any other poet in ancient Israel—but also a very bold thinker, not hesitating to challenge some of the essential ideas long cherished in Hebrew tradition. The boldness of the poetry is a necessary vehicle for the boldness of the thought. Poetry of the first order of originality is a way of enabling us to see the world with fresh eyes. It is worth going back to a notion promulgated by the Russian Formalists a century ago, that what literature in general does is to shake us out of what had become complacent, unseeing perception through what they called "defamiliarization," thereby bringing us back to the realities we had ceased to experience, making us feel anew the stoniness of the stone. The poetry of the Voice from the Whirlwind does this on a philosophical level, serving, I would say, as the Bible's ultimate defamiliarizer. As countless readers have complained, it does not really provide an answer for the dilemma of unwarranted suffering under a supposedly just God. That dilemma has no real answer, for there is no way of explaining why an innocent child should die of cancer or a benevolent woman perish in a fire with all her family. What the poetry does accomplish is to carry us away in its sweep, in the brilliance of its riveting and sometimes startling imagery, to see the world freshly, prodding us to let go of our habitual notions of man as the master of nature and the measure of all things, to realize that contradiction and anomaly and even violence are at the heart of reality—in sum, to accept the limitations of human imagination. We need to take in the power of the poetry in order to have a full sense of the originality of the thought.

AUTHOR-AUDIENCE DISCUSSION

AUDIENCE MEMBER: I'm curious about what dating you would assign to the Book of Job. Because you've alluded to Job borrowing some from Aramaic. There are some scholars that place the start of the use of Aramaic and Hebrew poetry to the exile. But there are other folks who say that Job is the earliest book of the Old Testament. Yeah. So, I'm really curious as to how you would deal with the whole history of Job.

ROBERT ALTER: I think it's totally unsustainable to date Job early. The presence of Aramaic in his poetry is one strong indication of that. And there's also another kind of lexical illustration. For example, the way you say *words* in Job is *millim*, which afterward became the standard Hebrew word for *words* and it's the modern Hebrew word for *words*. In the preexilic period, *millim* doesn't exist. Instead we have *devarim*. The Ten Commandments are actually called *asseret hadibrot* or *asseret devarim*. Given the linguistic evidence, of which this is a small example. there is no possibility that it's early. I would say it's probably the composition of the fifth century B.C.E., the 400s. Now, I will add to that a general comment about this period. In the first Israelite Commonwealth, say from about the year 1000 or a little bit after that until the destruction of the kingdom in 586, there was relative uniformity in literary form. I mean, there were of course differences between sources. Deuteronomy is quite different stylistically from the earlier Hebrew texts, but the same literary conventions recur in all the narratives. And I wouldn't say there's an absolute ideological unanimity because Deuteronomy introduces some new ideas, particularly the notion of the centrality of the cult in Jerusalem, which was not a general idea in the centuries before Deuteronomy. Deuteronomy is from the late seventh century B.C.E. But as I said, there is a relative linguistic and stylistic literary uniformity in these texts from the First Commonwealth period. Then in what scholars call the Late Biblical Period, which begins in the Babylonian exile, you have a kind of explosion of new literary forms. For example, there is nothing like the Book of Esther, nothing like Ecclesiastes (*Qohelet*), nothing like Job in the earlier texts. And this is not only an explosion of literary form, but also, certainly for Job and Ecclesiastes, it's an explosion of thinking about the world. As we've seen, the anthropocentrism of the earlier period, which all currents reflect, is challenged radically by Job. By the way, that's one of the reasons why the Book of Job, not just Leviathan, appealed to Herman Melville when he wrote *Moby-Dick,* because *Moby-Dick* is a radically anti-anthropocentric book, and that's something in Job that jibed with Melville's vision of the world. For these reasons, Job has to be from the later period.

AUDIENCE MEMBER: Given our overall society now, how would (biblical) poetry assist us in bringing some kind of peace in this journey that we're all going through? If I'm looking at Job, I'm seeing a human person crying out, being lost in the wilderness, just seeking guidance. And being subjective in his voice, he's looking for this "objective truth." He's seeking it out. And he wants guidance. It was only when God responded, and in God's authoritative voice, which is what we need in society, so to speak, it's like He says, "I am the authority. I am who am." Even the whole thing of creation is like, it's so evident that there is an authority figure, there is God who exists, who has created all this for mankind. So the bottom line for me is, poetry is beautiful. There's a rhythmic intensification in it, but as a woman, as a mother, a daughter, so to speak, and descended from the tribe of Joseph, I prefer to have truth, objective truth, in this whole maze that we're all traveling as human beings. So I don't know if it's a question or if it's just a statement, but it's just, poetry does serve a purpose. And there's beauty in it.

JOB

ROBERT ALTER: I really appreciate your remarks. I would say a couple of things. I spoke about the prophets and poetry earlier. But focusing on Job, I think that believing people and then people who are searching, who may not be sure they believe anything, should not be excluded from those who are searching for meaning in the Bible. You say "need." Okay. We all need comfort. There are many hardships in life and life is full of loss. My beloved wife of forty-nine years died three years ago, and I still can't get over it. So we certainly all need comfort. But we also need challenges. We need to know that things may not always be harmonious, that there are contradictions and challenges to our need for comfort. And since you eloquently speak about your feeling about things as a mother—I have four kids, of course, all long grown—I think the vivid poetic affirmation of birth and nurturing is so central in God's response to Job that that is something that can speak to everyone, especially to mothers.

AUDIENCE MEMBER: In Samuel there's a story about King Saul. Here's a popular verse being sung that Saul had slain his thousands, and David tens of thousands—there's your inflation for you. Was Saul outraged because he was ignorant of the proper structure of deeper poetry?

ROBERT ALTER: I think all kinds of silly things have been said by scholars over the years. There was one who wrote a little book, and not a very good book, on biblical poetry in which he said exactly what you say now. He proposed that Saul simply missed the signal that this is the way a line of biblical poetry is supposed to be structured. You move in the first half of the line to the second half from thousands to tens of thousands, as I observed at the beginning of my talk. But I think it's silly to imagine that is all that's involved because the necessity of form doesn't exclude meaning. So here, in fact, the form is significantly adapted to meaning. That is, the young women of Israel who are chanting this line are following the logic of line structure, but they're saying something that they mean. What they're saying is: "Saul's pretty great. He's won battles for us. But he's not as great as David." Understandably, this is a declaration that drives Saul to distraction.

AUDIENCE MEMBER: I see the parallelism between chapter 3 and 39. But I feel like I'm missing God's voice in the question of pain. Do we actually see where pain is addressed there, since Job was in pain? Or is that absent? And, if so, why?

ROBERT ALTER: That's a tough one, I have to admit. That is, I think many readers—believers and nonbelievers—have not been entirely happy with the ending of Job. We've witnessed so vividly and concretely the pain Job endured that one could reasonably say, OK, we see that the world is more dynamic and contradictory and grand than Job has imagined. But, still, what about all the terrible suffering he's undergone? And I would say that the Job poet, as great as he is as a poet and as bold as he is as a thinker, doesn't entirely answer that, and perhaps there is no real answer to unwarranted suffering.

AUDIENCE MEMBER: We need to grasp the Book of Job as a very powerful description of creation. Now, I'm not interested in authority, so much as romance. I think the ones who end up believing through pain and suffering, and the degradation of our nature in our world today, and other problems that we face, that "the romantic" is the one who survives, the one who falls in love; and this poetry makes me fall in love with God. I see him as so much more than I can imagine. And poetry helps you do that. If you have lists of rules and authorities that tell you how everything is, you can only go so far. But a surrender to this kind of God is possible when I see this beauty in the writing.

Robert Alter: That's a very eloquent and moving response to the Book of Job, and I thank you for it. I would just add this, that by and large—you can find a few minor exceptions—but by and large, biblical poets are not all that interested in nature. But this is not true of the Job poet. This rapt attention to nature is not only manifested in the God speech at the end of the book but, along the way, when in the poet's exploring a particular image or comparison, he will evoke the rainy season, the sprouting of grass in the spring, the cycle of seasons. This is something other biblical poets very rarely do. His was an amazingly capacious imagination, I would say. And I can see that this imagination has gotten through to you, which is very nice.

Audience member: I had thought the same as the previous questioners had thought about Job and God's response. However, now looking at it poetically, even more deeply, and God's response, I see now that God is softening his response through the poetry. You need it to soften his response. And to actually get Job to go deeper in his "go deeper," "do you remember why." I know in your suffering and sorrow, you can't see why. And I am asking you to go deeper. And through the poetry is the only way to go deeper into why his suffering is so important, and why he needs to look deeper into the meaning of

God, and to remember what God has taught him from the very beginning. Thank you.

ROBERT ALTER: I thank you for that. And what I would like to add to your comment is simply the dimension of powerful visuality. I don't have the whole text of Job in front of me, but when Job speaks after he listens to the speech from the whirlwind, he says—I don't remember it word for word, so this is a loose paraphrase—"I had heard word of you. But now I have seen," and the "seeing" is something that poetry has brought him to do.

AUDIENCE MEMBER: The question that I have is more curiosity. Going back to an example in Job 3:4–8. And they're all comparing the light, the day, the night, all of that, and then it throws in Leviathan. But yet at the same time in the King James it throws in "mourning" instead of Leviathan. Just an explanation for that.

ROBERT ALTER: The explanation is that this is simply an error. Let me say this. I am an admirer of the King James Version. I'm much happier with the King James version than with all the translations done in various denominational groups in the second half of the twentieth century by ecclesiastical-academic committees, by scholars with plenty of credentials. You know, they had advanced degrees in biblical studies—in England from Oxford and Cambridge, and in this country from Yale and the Harvard Divinity School, and so on. But they unfortunately had a tin ear for English. Really, there's sometimes a mangling of English idioms in their translations, an offensive mingling of different levels of diction, so that half a verse sounds like a government directive and the other half like the daily newspaper. Whereas the King James translators were in touch with the literary English of their time and had a great ear for language. The leading figure among the translators was Launcelot Andrewes, who was the bishop of London, and he was a great prose stylist. We know this because his sermons were published, and they are available to read. So, in many ways, the King James Version has real resonance and is an impressive literary achievement. But I would say this, that the knowledge of Hebrew among Christian Hebraists at the beginning of the seventeenth century though admirable was imperfect. As a result. they scrambled certain things. They got the meanings of words wrong, they got confused by the syntax and the idiomatic usage.

I'll give you an example outside of Job. In the covenant between the cut animal parts in Genesis between Abraham and God, the King James Version has a line that reads like this: "and lo, an horror of great darkness fell upon him." Now, this makes Abraham our forefather afraid of the dark. But in fact, what the Hebrew says is a "great dark dread." And here is the problem: the word that means dark, *ḥasheikha,* can either be an adjective meaning dark, or it can be a noun, meaning darkness. What they did reflects a confusion about the syntax. They read the Hebrew word as darkness and therefore came out with this wrong meaning. A different misunderstanding of the Hebrew led to their failure to translate "Leviathan" as it should have been. To begin with, *levaya,* in the sense of funeral or mourning, is not really a biblical word. It's a rabbinic Hebrew term. And they didn't distinguish clearly between the two strata of the language. And then they also let their perception of the grammar lapse a bit here. They didn't realize that what they construed as a feminine, possessive suffix, couldn't be that because there is no feminine referent in the verse. The mistake, which I have to say is egregious, resulted from the limits of their knowledge of Hebrew.

Audience member: Hello. I have a question about form. I guess the way that I read Job is kind of like a spotlight. There's a spotlight on Job in his death wish. It's all about me, like, "Woe is me." And then the spotlight kind of shifts in chapter 38 to God, where God is asking questions, and he's saying, it's actually me, like, "Where were you? Oh, you weren't there, because it was me." But then in 39, it feels like the tone shifts where it's not. I feel like the questions get farther and farther apart. It's not so much God saying, "Who are you? Who am I?" It changes even in pronouns to more like they, he, she. I'm curious, is it just like you said, so that the poet can show off? "Look at how many things I can do?" Is it meant to ground us back in the majesties of nature? If Job is hearing this response, what are we supposed to think of it? Because it feels a little ranty and like in an opposite direction.

Robert Alter: I think that this poet felt—and my response goes back to an earlier question/comment about nature and the love of nature—that this poet felt very deeply that nature was an awesome realm. In this instance, I suppose I mean "awesome" in the modern, colloquial sense. And so, once he had given the big picture of light and darkness, creation, winds sweeping over the world and so forth, he then zooms in to the animal kingdom. And he evokes all these creatures. Now, the war horse, OK, probably he had a sense as a poet, this was a great opportunity to show what I can do. But it does also fit in with his representation of all these other powerful creatures in the natural world who manifest their strength and vitality.

AUDIENCE MEMBER: OK, I have a short anecdote here. I'm professor of Old Testament at Biola University. Before that, I was in Canada, teaching Old Testament, and we had some guests on our campus who had lived and worked in China. The Chinese government decided that they must be spies. And so they arrested them and imprisoned them for over a year. And over the course of that year, they experienced repeated torture, and attempts to extract information. And at one point early in their imprisonment, someone brought them their Bibles, and I'm not sure how that miracle happened. But all they had was their Bible. So it was they were being tortured or they were reading their Bible for a whole year. And so I had to take the opportunity. I said, Julia, could you share with my students? What was the part of the Bible that was most precious to you in this season of suffering? And I was flabbergasted when she responded, Job chapter 3.

ROBERT ALTER: Oh, wow. This is a remarkable story and testimony to the Job poet's power to represent suffering,

AUDIENCE MEMBER: I said, "Please help us understand why." And she said, "I had never been in such the depths of despair as I was during that time, and I found this chapter in the Bible that perfectly expressed my own suffering, and my own feeling about my life." And she found a sense of solidarity with Job. And so I feel like this is a response partly to your comment earlier about where is suffering in this book. There's something, even though God doesn't respond explicitly to Job's suffering, his response preserves the conversation. And so somehow it makes space for us to express these hardships and helps us to feel that we're a little bit less alone. So I just I thought I'd share that and also wanted to say thank you. I've been using your translation of Job 3 in my classes every year when I teach Job, and we just read through this luscious poetry, and I think it opens up space for students to think, "Could I talk to God like that? Could I pray this honestly?" What would it look like if I didn't just use canned prayers, but if I actually expressed how much despair or darkness I'm feeling. So I wanted to thank you for kind of opening that up for my students.

Robert Alter: Thank you for that remark. It is an amazing anecdote that you tell. What a reminder, by the way. In Hasidic tradition, there's this concept of *chutzpah klappei shemaya* which means "chutzpah toward the heavens," meaning God. And that is legitimated as an understandable human response when the human person is being authentic to his or her own experience of outrage and suffering.

Audience member: So at the risk of going from the sublime to the potentially ridiculous—and prefacing this by saying I'm not a fan of numerology, because I'm sure a numerologist can come up with just about anything he wants—but I'm curious whether in the selection of vocabulary used in Job or in other biblical literature there's been any sensible numerological basis that you know about?

Robert Alter: I don't think so. Numerology on the Bible has attracted a lot of cranks. I've read a couple of articles by fairly serious people who say, "Well, there's a pattern of sevens here, or there's a pattern of tens there," but it doesn't seem convincing to me.

AUDIENCE MEMBER: Similar to the figure of Daniel and the Book of Daniel, is the "Job" named here before the Book of Job was written, or after?

ROBERT ALTER: Oh, definitely before. That is, especially if you think about the folktale frame. Obviously, there was a story something like this circulating in ancient Israel. We don't necessarily think it was identical with the story we have in the canonical text, but there was some sort of story, probably in oral tradition, about a wise and pious man named Job who went through a period of suffering and then was rewarded for his virtue. Subsequently, the poetic genius who composed the body of the Book of Job took that story, broke it open, and made it the frame for his poetic book. Maybe he modified the traditional tale to some extent, but in any case it's not a perfect fit with the Book of Job because, as many people have remarked, it doesn't seem plausible that God would agree to this peculiar wager with the Adversary, and the fairytale happy ending doesn't seem to belong to the poet's complex and unflinching vision of the world —that ending in which all Job's dead children are replaced. We know that there's never replacement for lives lost. Job, moreover, at the end has these three beautiful daughters who have names evocative of femininity and attractiveness, still another flourish of the happy ending. So there was an old story about Job, as I've said. Since it probably circulated just orally, we'll never know its exact formulation. In any case, it was picked up by the poet as a frame for something entirely original. And Daniel, also some sort of legendary figure in Israelite culture, was adopted by a writer in the second century B.C.E. and made the protagonist of the book that bears his name.

Audience member: Thank you, Professor, for your exposition this morning. Can you address the thing that always gets me with Job, the invitation to "gird your loins and face me like a man" before he goes on to talk about how vast and wonderful he is as God? Is that hyperbolic flourish from the poet? Or is that a more intimate understanding of the Hebrew that they were made in the likeness and image of God and could therefore get in the octagon with God? What are your thoughts?

Robert Alter: I think what God is saying in "gird your loins" is that "I'm about to deliver a series of truths to you. And they are going to be hard truths, not all of which will be easily assimilable. So now summon all your fortitude, and listen to what I have to say."

Father Hugh of St. Michael's Abbey: Professor Alter, we're very grateful to you for having given us such a serious reading of the scriptures. I think in the future, when I read certain passages, I'm going to hear your serene and erudite voice in the background just taking me through. It's an important experience for me, I think. And, of course, that love for the beauty of God's Word and its understanding is something that we have to take with us and hopefully inspire some of our young men to learn Hebrew. So I started out with Hebrew in college but didn't continue it. And now when I'm attending this, I really regret it, but nothing to be done now. You can't do everything in life.

HENRY CHADWICK AND THOMAS C. ODEN

HENRY CHADWICK (1920–2008) was a British theologian and Church of England priest. A leading historian of the early church, Chadwick was appointed Regius Professor at both the universities of Oxford and Cambridge. He was general editor of the Oxford History of the Christian Church, and Oxford Early Christian Texts. His publications included *Origen: Contra Celsum*; *Early Christian Thought and the Classical Tradition*; *Saint Augustine: Confessions* (translation and notes); and *The Early Church* (The Penguin History of the Church).

THOMAS C. ODEN (1931–2016) was an American Methodist theologian, often regarded as the father of the paleo-orthodox theological movement. He was Henry Anson Buttz Professor of Theology at The Theological School, Drew University, and the general editor of the multivolume patristic *Ancient Christian Commentary on Scripture*. The author of numerous books, including a highly regarded three-volume systematic theology, he also served as a general editor for Ancient Christian Texts and as director of the Center for Early African Christianity.

St. Michael's Abbey

Nestled in Southern California's Santiago Canyon, St. Michael's Abbey is regarded as one of the largest communities of the world-wide Norbertine Order. The Abbey's story begins in 1957 when seven Hungarian refugee priests fled from the Communist suppression of their abbey in Csorna, Hungary, and immigrated to Southern California to establish a small monastery in 1961. Today, St. Michael's Abbey has grown to over sixty priests and over forty seminarians in formation. Immersed in a tradition enduring over nine hundred years, the Norbertine Order is named after St. Norbert of Xanten (d. 1134), whose conviction that clerical reform and church renewal were needed in his day through the life and work of monastic communities. St. Augustine of Hippo's rule for clerics, which St. Norbert adopted, continues to be followed among the Norbertines to this day in their communal living and vows of poverty, celibacy, and obedience. St. Michael's Abbey is home to a special collections library that includes papers and fifteen thousand volumes from Henry Chadwick's personal collection, as well as Thomas C. Oden's rare book collection. To learn more about the Abbey, visit stmichaelsabbey.com.

www.ingramcontent.com/pod-product-compliance
Lightning Source LLC
Chambersburg PA
CBHW061810070526
44586CB00024B/2793